TAIWAN TRAVEL GUIDE

**An Ultimate Manual To Essential &
Updated Travel Information, Must-See
Destinations, Time To Visit, Top
Accommodations & Transportation To
Discover Taipei, The Capital & More**

WELCOME TO

TAIWAN

Nestled in the heart of East Asia, Taiwan is a fascinating island with a rich history, vibrant culture, and stunning landscapes. The story of Taiwan's formation is a blend of geological wonders and human ingenuity.

HOW TO USE THIS GUIDE

Welcome to the "Taiwan Travel Guide ," your ultimate companion for exploring the rich tapestry of Taiwan's landscapes, culture, and cuisine. This guide is meticulously crafted to provide you with essential and updated travel information, must-see destinations, and practical tips to make your journey seamless and unforgettable. Here's how to navigate through this book and make the most of your travel planning.

- **Overview of the Book**

This travel guide is structured to take you through Taiwan's multifaceted offerings in a logical and user-friendly manner. Each section is designed to provide detailed insights and practical advice, ensuring you have everything you need for a well-rounded and enriching travel experience.

- **How to Use This Guide**

This introductory section helps you understand the layout of the book and how to utilize each chapter effectively.

- **Welcome to Taiwan**

A warm introduction to Taiwan, setting the stage for your adventure.

- **Chapter One: Overview of Taiwan**

Gain a foundational understanding of Taiwan's geography and climate, and discover why it is a must-visit destination.

- **Chapter Two: Essential Travel Information**

Learn about the best times to visit, entry requirements, currency matters, and language tips to ensure a smooth start to your trip.

- **Chapter Three: Getting to & Around Taiwan: Transportation Options**

Explore various transportation options for getting to Taiwan and navigating the island, including public transportation, car rentals, and driving tips.

- **Chapter Four: Time to Visit**

Discover Taiwan's seasonal highlights, major events and festivals, and get recommendations on the ideal duration of your stay.

- **Chapter Five: 5-Day Itinerary for Taiwan**

A detailed day-by-day itinerary to help you experience the best of Taiwan in five days, from Taipei to Kenting National Park.

- **Chapter Six: Must-See Destinations**

A curated list of Taiwan's top attractions, including Taipei 101, Sun Moon Lake, and Taroko Gorge.

- **Chapter Seven: Discovering the Cultural Capital**

Delve into Taipei's vibrant culture, shopping, dining, and nightlife.

- **Chapter Eight: Where to Stay: Top Accommodations**

Find recommendations for luxury hotels, boutique villas, cozy bed and breakfasts, and budget-friendly options.

- **Chapter Nine: Where to Eat: Culinary Delights**

Explore Taiwan's culinary scene, from fine dining to charming cafés and night markets, and discover local dishes and hidden gems.

- **Chapter Ten: Practical Tips and Recommendations**

Essential advice on packing, safety, local etiquette, and sustainable travel practices.

- **Navigating the Book**

Each chapter is divided into sections and subsections to help you find information quickly and easily. The book is designed for both comprehensive reading and quick referencing, so whether you're planning your trip from scratch or looking for specific details on the go, this guide has you covered.

- **Features and Offers**

- **Detailed Itineraries**: Follow our expertly crafted itineraries to maximize your time and experience the best Taiwan has to offer.

- **Insider Tips**: Benefit from local insights and tips that you won't find in standard travel guides.
- **Comprehensive Listings**: Discover a wide range of accommodations, dining options, and must-see attractions to suit every budget and interest.
- **Practical Advice:** From visa requirements to language tips, get all the practical information you need for a hassle-free trip.
- **Cultural Insights**: Learn about Taiwan's rich cultural heritage, festivals, and customs to enhance your travel experience.
- **Sustainable Travel:** Find recommendations on how to travel responsibly and sustainably, minimizing your environmental impact.

By using this guide, you will have a well-rounded resource at your fingertips, ensuring that your trip to Taiwan is not only enjoyable but also enriching and memorable. Whether you're a first-time visitor or a seasoned traveler, the "Taiwan Travel Guide " is your essential companion for discovering the beauty and diversity of this incredible island.

TABLE OF CONTENTS

WELCOME TO TAIWAN

Nestled in the heart of East Asia, Taiwan is a fascinating island with a rich history, vibrant culture, and stunning landscapes. The story of Taiwan's formation is a blend of geological wonders and human ingenuity. Formed by the collision of the Philippine Sea Plate and the Eurasian Plate, Taiwan boasts rugged mountains, lush forests, and stunning coastlines. But it's the island's cultural and historical evolution that truly captivates visitors.

In the early 17th century, the Dutch East India Company established a trading post on the island, marking the beginning of Taiwan's integration into global trade networks. Later, the island came under the rule of the Ming loyalist Koxinga, who expelled the Dutch and established a base for resisting the Qing dynasty. Taiwan was later incorporated into the Qing Empire and then ceded to Japan in 1895, only to be retroceded to China after World War II. Each of these periods left an indelible mark on Taiwan's culture, architecture, and society.

The name "Taiwan" is believed to have originated from the indigenous Siraya people who called the area "Taoyuan," meaning "foreigners." Over time, this name evolved and was adopted by the various ruling entities, eventually becoming the island's official name.

- **Discovering Taiwan's Rich Past and Present**

My name is Kendall Dora, and my journey to becoming a travel guidebook author began with a deep love for exploration and storytelling. My fascination with Taiwan started during a spontaneous trip several years ago. From the moment I stepped off the plane, I was entranced by the island's unique blend of ancient traditions and modern innovation.

Taiwan is a place where bustling night markets coexist with serene temples, where the echoes of history can be heard in the clamor of contemporary life. It's a destination that offers something for everyone, whether you're a history buff, a foodie, an adventurer, or simply seeking a new experience.

- **Why Visit Taiwan?**

Taiwan's allure lies in its contrasts. Picture this: you're standing at the top of Taipei 101, one of the tallest buildings in the world, with a panoramic view of a sprawling, modern metropolis. Yet, just a short drive away, you can find yourself hiking through the verdant trails of Yangmingshan National Park, surrounded by hot springs and volcanic landscapes.

One of the highlights of my travels in Taiwan was visiting the National Palace Museum in Taipei, which houses one of the largest collections of Chinese art and artifacts in the world. Walking through its halls, you can almost feel the weight of history, from ancient jade carvings to exquisite porcelain and calligraphy.

And then there are the superlative restaurants. Taiwan is a gastronomic paradise, where every meal is an adventure. From the world-famous Din Tai Fung, known for its delicate xiaolongbao (soup dumplings), to the myriad street food stalls offering everything from stinky tofu to bubble tea, the island's culinary scene is second to none.

- **Experiencing Taiwan's Design and Innovation**

Taiwan is also a hub of creativity and innovation. Design-led stores and boutiques abound, particularly in the capital city of Taipei. The Songshan Cultural and Creative

Park, for example, is a testament to Taiwan's thriving design industry. Once a tobacco factory, it has been transformed into a creative hub where artists and designers showcase their work. Browsing through these stores, you'll find everything from sleek, minimalist homeware to quirky, avant-garde fashion.

- **Why You Should Buy This Book**

With "TAIWAN TRAVEL GUIDE : An Ultimate Manual To Essential & Updated Travel Information, Must-See Destinations, Time To Visit, Top Accommodations & Transportation To Discover Taipei, The Capital & More," I've poured my extensive knowledge and personal experiences into creating a comprehensive and detailed guidebook. This isn't just a collection of facts and figures; it's a curated experience designed to help you uncover the magic of Taiwan.

One of the standout features of this guide is the 4-5 day itinerary, meticulously crafted to give you a taste of Taiwan's diverse offerings. Whether you're arriving in Taipei and exploring its many wonders, venturing to the serene Sun Moon Lake, or hiking through the dramatic Taroko Gorge, this itinerary ensures you don't miss a thing.

With this guide in hand, you'll have everything you need to plan and enjoy an extraordinary trip to Taiwan. Whether it's your first visit or you're returning to explore more of what the island has to offer, "TAIWAN TRAVEL GUIDE " is your ultimate companion for discovering the beauty, culture, and wonder of this remarkable destination.

ONE

OVERVIEW OF TAIWAN AND IT NEIGHBORHOOD

GEOGRAPHY AND CLIMATE

Taiwan, an island nation in East Asia, offers a captivating blend of natural beauty, rich history, and vibrant culture. Its geographical location, diverse topography, and unique cultural heritage make it an enticing destination for travelers seeking both adventure and enlightenment.

- **History**

Taiwan's history is a mosaic of indigenous heritage, colonial influences, and modern development. The island was originally inhabited by indigenous Austronesian tribes, whose presence dates back thousands of years. In the 17th century, Taiwan became a focal point for colonial powers, with the Dutch and Spanish establishing settlements. The Ming loyalist Koxinga later expelled the Dutch, setting the stage for Chinese influence under the Qing dynasty. Taiwan was ceded to Japan in 1895 and reverted to Chinese rule after World War II. Each era left a distinct mark on Taiwan's cultural and architectural landscape.

- **Geography and Climate**

Situated off the southeastern coast of China, Taiwan is bounded by the East China Sea to the north, the Philippine Sea to the east, the Luzon Strait to the south, and the Taiwan Strait to the west. The island's topography is diverse, featuring rugged mountains, rolling hills, and fertile plains. The Central Mountain Range runs the length of the island, providing dramatic landscapes and lush forests.

Taiwan's climate is generally subtropical, with mild winters and hot, humid summers. The island experiences a monsoon season from May to September, bringing heavy rains, particularly on the east coast. Typhoons are common during late summer and early autumn, adding a dynamic element to the weather patterns.

- **Culture and People**

The culture of Taiwan is a vibrant tapestry woven from indigenous traditions, Chinese influences, and Japanese colonial legacies. The indigenous tribes, such as the Amis, Atayal, and Paiwan, contribute to Taiwan's rich cultural heritage. Each tribe has its own unique customs, festivals, and artistic traditions. The Amis, for example, are known for their vibrant harvest festivals and intricate beadwork, while the Atayal are celebrated for their weaving and facial tattoo traditions.

Taiwan's cultural heritage is also evident in its traditional art forms, including intricate wood carvings, pottery, and weaving. Notable symbols of native art, such as Taiwan's ornate pottery and Atayal's geometric textiles, reflect the deep connection between the people and their land.

The people of Taiwan are renowned for their warmth, hospitality, and resilience. The population is predominantly Han Chinese, with significant Hakka and indigenous communities. This ethnic diversity contributes to Taiwan's rich cultural mosaic. The Taiwanese way of life is characterized by a harmonious blend of traditional values and modern dynamism. Family ties are strong, and traditional festivals, such as Lunar New Year and the Mid-Autumn Festival, are celebrated with great fervor.

Communication in Taiwan is facilitated by Mandarin Chinese, the official language, though Taiwanese Hokkien and Hakka are also widely spoken. English is commonly used in business and tourism, making it relatively easy for visitors to navigate.

- **Vibrant Heritage**

Taiwan's vibrant heritage is showcased in its lively festivals, bustling night markets, and historic temples. The Lantern Festival, held annually in Pingxi, is a mesmerizing spectacle of light and color, while the Dragon Boat Festival features exciting races and cultural performances. Taiwan's temples, such as the Longshan Temple in Taipei and the Fo Guang Shan Monastery in Kaohsiung, offer a glimpse into the island's spiritual life and architectural splendor.

The island's coastal areas and rich marine culture are integral to its identity. The picturesque fishing ports, seafood markets, and marine reserves highlight Taiwan's connection to the sea. The Penghu Archipelago, with its stunning basalt formations and crystal-clear waters, is a testament to the island's geological and ecological diversity.

Taiwan is a land of contrasts and confluences, where ancient traditions coexist with modern innovation. Its geographical diversity, rich cultural heritage, and the warmth of its people make it a compelling destination. Whether you're exploring the bustling streets of Taipei, hiking through the serene mountains, or immersing yourself in the island's vibrant festivals, Taiwan offers an enriching and unforgettable experience.

WHY TAIWAN IS A MUST-VISIT DESTINATION

Taiwan, often referred to as the "Heart of Asia," is an island that offers a captivating blend of natural beauty, rich cultural heritage, and modern sophistication. This unique destination is a must-visit for travelers seeking an unforgettable experience. Here are some of the most exciting reasons why Taiwan should be at the top of your travel list.

- **Stunning Natural Landscapes**

Taiwan's diverse topography means that stunning natural landscapes are never far away. The island boasts majestic mountains, lush forests, and breathtaking coastlines. One of the most iconic natural wonders is Taroko Gorge, a marble-walled canyon that offers awe-inspiring views and thrilling hiking trails. Alishan National Scenic Area is another must-see, famous for its sunrise views, ancient forests, and scenic railway.

For beach lovers, Taiwan's coastline is dotted with beautiful beaches and crystal-clear waters. Kenting National Park in the south is particularly popular, known for its vibrant coral reefs and sandy shores. The Penghu Archipelago, with its stunning basalt formations and serene beaches, is a hidden gem waiting to be explored.

- **Rich Cultural Heritage**

Taiwan's cultural heritage is a tapestry woven from indigenous traditions, Chinese influences, and Japanese colonial legacies. The island is home to a myriad of temples, shrines, and historical sites. Longshan Temple in Taipei is a beautiful example of traditional Chinese architecture and a hub of religious activity. The National Palace Museum, also in Taipei, houses one of the largest collections of Chinese art and artifacts in the world, offering a deep dive into the region's history.

Festivals are an integral part of Taiwanese culture. The Lantern Festival, held in Pingxi, is a magical event where thousands of sky lanterns are released into the night sky. The Dragon Boat Festival features exciting boat races and cultural performances, celebrating the island's maritime heritage.

- **Culinary Delights**

Taiwan is a food lover's paradise. Its culinary scene is renowned for its diversity and quality. Night markets are a highlight, offering a variety of street foods that are both delicious and affordable. Shilin Night Market in Taipei is one of the largest and most famous, with stalls selling everything from stinky tofu to bubble tea.

For those seeking a more refined dining experience, Taiwan is home to several Michelin-starred restaurants. Din Tai Fung, famous for its xiaolongbao (soup dumplings), has garnered international acclaim. The island also offers a wealth of seafood, thanks to its coastal location, with dishes like oyster omelets and grilled squid being local favorites.

- **Modern Sophistication**

While Taiwan is steeped in tradition, it is also a hub of modern sophistication. Taipei 101, once the tallest building in the world, is an architectural marvel that offers panoramic views of the city from its observation deck. The capital city, Taipei, is a bustling metropolis with a vibrant nightlife, high-end shopping districts, and innovative technology hubs.

Taiwan's design and creative industries are thriving, with areas like Songshan Cultural and Creative Park showcasing the best of Taiwanese innovation and artistry. This former tobacco factory has been transformed into a space where artists and designers can display their work, making it a must-visit for those interested in contemporary art and design.

- **Welcoming People**

One of the most compelling reasons to visit Taiwan is its people. Taiwanese are known for their warmth, friendliness, and hospitality. Whether you're navigating the streets of Taipei or exploring rural villages, you'll find that locals are eager to help and share their culture with visitors. This welcoming spirit makes Taiwan a particularly enjoyable destination for solo travelers and families alike.

- **Adventure and Relaxation**

Taiwan offers the perfect balance of adventure and relaxation. For adrenaline junkies, activities such as paragliding, surfing, and mountain climbing are readily available. Taiwan's hot springs provide a perfect way to unwind after a day of exploration. Beitou Hot Springs in Taipei is one of the most accessible, offering a range of bathhouses and public baths.

Taiwan is a destination that truly has it all. From its stunning natural landscapes and rich cultural heritage to its vibrant culinary scene and modern sophistication, the island offers an array of experiences that cater to all types of travelers. Whether you're seeking adventure, relaxation, or a deep cultural immersion, Taiwan promises a journey that is as enriching as it is unforgettable. So pack your bags and get ready to discover the wonders of Taiwan – a destination that will leave you with memories to last a lifetime.

TWO

ESSENTIAL TRAVEL INFORMATION

BEST TIME TO VISIT

Choosing the best time to visit Taiwan can significantly enhance your travel experience, as the island offers different attractions and events throughout the year. Taiwan's subtropical climate ensures that it remains a year-round destination, but certain months offer more favorable weather and exciting events.

- **Weather Overview**

Taiwan experiences four distinct seasons. Spring (March to May) is one of the best times to visit, with mild temperatures ranging from 20°C to 25°C (68°F to 77°F) and blooming cherry blossoms creating picturesque landscapes. This season is perfect for outdoor activities such as hiking in Taroko Gorge or exploring Alishan National Scenic Area.

Summer (June to August) brings hot and humid weather, with temperatures often exceeding 30°C (86°F). While this is also the typhoon season, the coastal areas and beaches in Kenting National Park and the Penghu Islands offer great opportunities for water sports and beach relaxation.

Autumn (September to November) is another excellent time to visit. The weather is comfortable, with temperatures between 22°C and 28°C (72°F to 82°F), and the typhoon risk diminishes. This season is ideal for exploring Taiwan's cultural sites and enjoying the vibrant fall foliage in places like Yangmingshan National Park.

Winter (December to February) is relatively mild, with temperatures ranging from 15°C to 20°C (59°F to 68°F) in the lower regions. However, it can get cooler in the mountains. Winter is also a great time to enjoy Taiwan's hot springs, particularly in Beitou and Wulai.

- **Popular Events**

Taiwan hosts numerous festivals and events that can enrich your visit. The Lantern Festival, held in February or March, is a spectacular event where thousands of lanterns illuminate the night sky. The Dragon Boat Festival in June features exciting boat races and traditional celebrations. In October, the Double Ten Day, Taiwan's National Day, is celebrated with grand parades and fireworks.

For a unique cultural experience, visit during the Ghost Festival in August, when various rituals and performances are held to honor deceased ancestors. Lastly, the Mid-Autumn Festival, usually in September, is a time for mooncakes, lantern displays, and family gatherings.

The best time to visit Taiwan depends on your weather preferences and interest in local events. Whether you seek the beauty of cherry blossoms in spring, the excitement of summer festivals, the comfortable autumn weather, or the cultural richness of winter, Taiwan has something to offer every traveler year-round.

ENTRY REQUIREMENTS AND VISA INFORMATION

When planning a trip to Taiwan, understanding the entry requirements and visa information is crucial for a smooth and hassle-free experience. Here's everything you need to know:

- **Visa-Free Entry**

Taiwan offers visa-free entry for citizens of several countries, including the United States, Canada, Australia, the European Union, Japan, South Korea, and many more. The duration of stay varies by country, generally ranging from 14 to 90 days. Travelers should ensure their passport is valid for at least six months beyond their intended departure date.

- **Visa-Exempt Program**

For visitors from countries not eligible for visa-free entry, Taiwan has a visa-exempt program. This program allows travelers to apply for a eVisa or a visa on arrival. The eVisa application can be completed online and is typically processed within three business days. It grants a stay of up to 30 days and is valid for three months from the date of issuance.

- **Visitor Visa**

For those requiring a longer stay or multiple entries, a visitor visa is available. This visa allows stays of up to 90 days and can be extended once for an additional 90 days. To apply, travelers need to submit an application form, a passport-sized photo, a valid passport, proof of onward travel, and evidence of sufficient funds. Applications can be submitted at a Taiwanese embassy or consulate.

- **Special Entry Permits**

Certain travelers, such as those visiting for business, study, or family reunification, may require special entry permits. These permits often require additional documentation, such as invitation letters or proof of enrollment.

- **Health and Safety Requirements**

Due to the COVID-19 pandemic, Taiwan has implemented health and safety measures for incoming travelers. These may include proof of vaccination, negative PCR test results, and mandatory quarantine periods. Travelers should check the latest requirements before their trip, as regulations can change rapidly.

- **Customs Regulations**

Travelers should also be aware of Taiwan's customs regulations. Items such as narcotics, firearms, and certain agricultural products are prohibited. Duty-free allowances include up to 200 cigarettes, 25 cigars, or 1 pound of tobacco, along with 1 liter of alcoholic beverages.

By understanding these entry requirements and visa options, travelers can ensure a smooth journey to Taiwan, allowing them to focus on enjoying all that this vibrant destination has to offer.

CURRENCY AND MONEY MATTERS

When traveling to Taiwan, understanding the local currency and money matters is essential for a smooth and enjoyable trip. Here's everything you need to know:

- **Local Currency**

The official currency of Taiwan is the New Taiwan Dollar (NTD or TWD), commonly referred to as the NT$. The currency comes in both coins and banknotes. Coins are available in denominations of 1, 5, 10, 20, and 50 NT$, while banknotes come in 100, 200, 500, 1000, and 2000 NT$.

- **Exchanging Money**

Currency exchange services are widely available in Taiwan. You can exchange money at banks, major hotels, and authorized money changers. Banks typically offer better exchange rates than hotels or exchange booths at airports. It's advisable to exchange some money upon arrival for immediate expenses, such as transportation or meals.

- **ATMs and Credit Cards**

ATMs are widely available throughout Taiwan, especially in urban areas. Most ATMs accept international cards affiliated with Visa, MasterCard, and other major networks. Be sure to inform your bank of your travel plans to avoid any issues with card usage abroad. Additionally, be aware of any foreign transaction fees your bank might charge.

Credit cards are commonly accepted in hotels, department stores, restaurants, and larger retail establishments. However, smaller shops, markets, and some rural areas may only accept cash. It's a good idea to carry some cash for small purchases and situations where credit cards aren't accepted.

- **Tipping Culture**

Tipping is not customary in Taiwan and is generally not expected. Service charges are often included in the bill at hotels and upscale restaurants. However, if you receive exceptional service and wish to leave a tip, it will certainly be appreciated.

- **Mobile Payments**

Taiwan has embraced mobile payment systems, such as Apple Pay, Google Pay, and local options like LINE Pay and JKOPay. These methods are convenient and widely accepted in urban areas, making transactions quick and easy.

- **Tax Refunds**

Tourists are eligible for tax refunds on purchases over a certain amount at participating stores. Look for the "Tax Refund Shopping" sign and keep your receipts. Refunds can be claimed at the airport upon departure.

By familiarizing yourself with Taiwan's currency and money matters, you can navigate financial transactions with ease, ensuring a stress-free and enjoyable travel experience.

LANGUAGE AND COMMUNICATION

Navigating language and communication in Taiwan can significantly enhance your travel experience. Here's everything you need to know:

- **Official Language**

Mandarin Chinese, also known as Standard Chinese, is the official language of Taiwan. It is the primary language used in government, education, and media. Mandarin is spoken by nearly everyone on the island, making it the most important language to know for communication purposes.

- **Dialects and Indigenous Languages**

In addition to Mandarin, you will encounter several dialects and languages. Taiwanese Hokkien (often simply referred to as Taiwanese) is widely spoken, especially among the older generation and in rural areas. Hakka is another common dialect, predominantly spoken by the Hakka ethnic group.

Taiwan is also home to several indigenous groups, each with its own distinct language. While these languages are less commonly spoken, they are an integral part of Taiwan's cultural heritage and are preserved and celebrated through various cultural initiatives.

- **English Proficiency**

English proficiency in Taiwan varies. In major cities like Taipei, Taichung, and Kaohsiung, many young people and professionals, especially those in the hospitality industry, can speak and understand English. Signage in tourist areas, public transportation, and major attractions often includes English translations, making it easier for English-speaking travelers to navigate.

However, in more rural areas, English speakers may be harder to find. Learning a few basic Mandarin phrases can go a long way in these regions. Simple greetings, numbers, and polite expressions can help you communicate more effectively and show respect for the local culture.

- **Useful Phrases**

Here are a few basic Mandarin phrases that can be helpful:

- **Hello:** 你好 (Nǐ hǎo)
- **Thank you:** 谢谢 (Xièxiè)
- **Yes:** 是 (Shì)
- **No:** 不是 (Bù shì)
- **Excuse me/Sorry:** 对不起 (Duìbùqǐ)
- **How much?:** 多少钱? (Duōshǎo qián?)

- **Communication Tools**

Smartphone apps can be invaluable for language translation and communication. Apps like Google Translate can translate text and speech in real-time, helping bridge the language gap. Additionally, many Taiwanese are familiar with messaging apps like LINE, which is widely used for communication.

- **Body Language and Etiquette**

Non-verbal communication also plays an important role. Taiwanese people value politeness and respect. A friendly smile, nod, or slight bow can convey gratitude and respect. Avoid using your index finger to point, as it is considered rude; use your whole hand instead.

By understanding the linguistic landscape and communication nuances of Taiwan, you can engage more deeply with locals and enrich your travel experience.

THREE

TRANSPORTATION OPTIONS

TRANSPORTATION OPTIONS IN TAIWAN

Taiwan offers a variety of transportation options that cater to both local commuters and international travelers. Here's a comprehensive guide to navigating the island:

- AIR TRAVEL

- **Domestic Flights**

Domestic flights are a quick way to travel between Taiwan's major cities and its outlying islands. Key airports include Taiwan Taoyuan International Airport (TPE), Taipei Songshan Airport (TSA), and Kaohsiung International Airport (KHH). Flights between Taipei and Kaohsiung take about an hour, with fares ranging from NT$1,500 to NT$3,000. Flights to outlying islands like Kinmen and Penghu are also available, offering convenient access to these scenic destinations.

- RAIL TRAVEL

- **Taiwan High-Speed Rail (THSR)**

The THSR is the fastest way to travel along Taiwan's west coast, connecting Taipei to Kaohsiung in about 1.5 to 2 hours. Major stops include Taoyuan, Hsinchu, Taichung,

Tainan, and Zuoying. Ticket prices from Taipei to Kaohsiung range from NT$1,490 for a standard seat to NT$2,440 for business class.

- **Taiwan Railways (TRA)**

The TRA operates an extensive network covering the entire island. Express trains like the Puyuma and Taroko offer faster services. A trip from Taipei to Hualien costs around NT$440 and takes about 2 hours. TRA trains are ideal for reaching smaller towns and scenic areas.

- METRO SYSTEMS

- **Taipei Metro (MRT)**

The Taipei MRT is efficient and covers the city and its suburbs with extensive lines. Fares range from NT$20 to NT$65. The MRT is a convenient way to explore Taipei's attractions and neighborhoods.

- **Kaohsiung Metro**

Kaohsiung's MRT is smaller but equally convenient, with fares ranging from NT$20 to NT$60. It connects major points in the city, including the airport and railway stations.

- BUS SERVICES

- **Long-Distance Buses**

Long-distance buses connect major cities and are an economical alternative to trains. Fares from Taipei to Kaohsiung are about NT$500 to NT$700. Companies like Kuo-Kuang and UBus offer comfortable and reliable services.

- **City Buses**

City buses are frequent and cover urban and suburban areas. Single-ride fares typically range from NT$15 to NT$30, payable with EasyCard or iPASS.

- **Taxis and Ride-Sharing**

Taxis are readily available in all major cities. In Taipei, the base fare is NT$70, with additional charges of NT$5 per 250 meters. Ride-sharing services like Uber are also available, offering a convenient and often cheaper alternative.

- **Bicycles**

Bike-sharing programs, such as YouBike in Taipei and Taichung, are popular. Renting a YouBike costs NT$10 for the first 30 minutes, providing an affordable and eco-friendly way to explore the cities.

- **Ferries**

Ferries connect Taiwan with its outlying islands like Penghu, Kinmen, and Matsu. The ferry from Kaohsiung to Penghu takes about 4-5 hours and costs between NT$1,000 and NT$2,000. Ferries are a scenic and enjoyable way to travel.

- **Car Rentals**

Renting a car offers flexibility for exploring Taiwan's scenic spots. Daily rental rates start at around NT$1,500. Renting scooters is also popular, with costs around NT$300 to NT$600 per day.

GETTING TO TAIWAN

Travelers can reach Taiwan by air, sea, and, to a limited extent, by land. Here's everything you need to know about each mode of transportation to ensure a smooth journey to this captivating island.

- BY AIR

- **Taiwan Taoyuan International Airport (TPE)**

Taiwan Taoyuan International Airport is the main gateway to Taiwan, located about 40 kilometers west of Taipei. It is the busiest airport in Taiwan and a major hub in East Asia. The airport website is [www.taoyuan-airport.com - https://www.taoyuan-airport.com).

- **Introduction and Airlines**

The airport is modern and well-equipped, offering a wide range of facilities, including duty-free shops, restaurants, lounges, and free Wi-Fi. Major airlines operating at Taoyuan International include China Airlines, EVA Air, Cathay Pacific, and United Airlines, offering numerous international routes.

- **Routes and Major Airports**

Taoyuan International connects to major cities worldwide, including Los Angeles, New York, Tokyo, Hong Kong, and London. It also serves numerous regional destinations within Asia.

- **Traveling from the Airport**

A taxi ride from Taoyuan International Airport to central Taipei takes approximately 45 minutes and costs around NT$1,200 to NT$1,500. Alternatively, the Taoyuan Airport MRT offers a more affordable option, taking about 35 minutes to reach Taipei Main Station for NT$160.

- **Other Airports**

Kaohsiung International Airport (KHH) and Taipei Songshan Airport (TSA) are other important airports. Kaohsiung serves southern Taiwan with flights to regional destinations, while Songshan caters to domestic flights and a few international routes, particularly to Japan and China.

- BY LAND

Traveling to Taiwan by land from neighboring countries is not feasible, as Taiwan is an island. However, visitors can combine land and sea travel. For example, travelers from mainland China can take a high-speed train to coastal cities like Xiamen or Fuzhou, then catch a ferry to Taiwan's outlying islands.

- BY SEA

- **Ferries and Ports**

Taiwan has several ports that receive international ferries. The Port of Keelung and the Port of Kaohsiung are the most significant. Ferries from Xiamen and Fuzhou in China arrive at these ports. While ferry travel is less common than air travel, it offers a unique experience, particularly for those exploring multiple destinations in the region.

- BY TRAIN

While there are no international train routes directly into Taiwan due to its island geography, Taiwan's domestic rail network is extensive and efficient. The Taiwan High-Speed Rail (THSR) connects major cities along the west coast, making travel within Taiwan quick and convenient. For those arriving by air, the THSR is a great way to explore the island.

With multiple ways to reach Taiwan, including modern airports, ferry services, and an efficient rail network, travelers have various options to start their Taiwanese adventure. Whether you arrive by air, sea, or a combination of land and sea routes, Taiwan's accessibility ensures a smooth beginning to your journey.

GETTING AROUND THE ISLAND

- **By Air**

While Taiwan is a relatively small island, there are domestic flights available for those looking to travel quickly between distant points. Domestic flights mainly operate between Taipei Songshan Airport (TSA), Taichung Airport (RMQ), Tainan Airport (TNN), and Kaohsiung International Airport (KHH). These flights are convenient for reaching remote islands such as Kinmen and Penghu. The average flight time between Taipei and Kaohsiung is about one hour, with ticket prices ranging from NT$1,500 to NT$3,000 depending on the airline and booking time.

- **By Bus**

Buses are a popular and economical way to travel around Taiwan. The island's extensive bus network includes long-distance coaches, city buses, and tourist shuttle buses. Long-distance coaches, operated by companies like Kuo-Kuang and UBus, connect major cities and tourist destinations. A one-way ticket from Taipei to Kaohsiung costs approximately NT$500 to NT$700. City buses in Taipei and other urban areas are frequent and affordable, with fares typically around NT$15 to NT$30, payable via EasyCard.

- **By Car & Motorcycle**

Renting a car or motorcycle offers flexibility and freedom to explore Taiwan at your own pace. Car rental prices start at around NT$1,500 per day for a compact car. International driving permits are accepted, and driving is on the right side of the road. For motorbike enthusiasts, renting a scooter is a popular option, especially in smaller

30

towns and islands like Penghu. Scooter rental costs around NT$300 to NT$600 per day. Fuel is relatively inexpensive, averaging NT$30 per liter.

- **By Boat**

Boat travel is ideal for reaching Taiwan's outlying islands. Ferries operate between the main island and destinations such as Penghu, Kinmen, and Matsu. The ferry from Kaohsiung to Penghu takes about four to five hours, with ticket prices ranging from NT$1,000 to NT$2,000 depending on the class of service. Ferries are also a scenic and enjoyable way to experience Taiwan's coastal beauty.

- **Hiring or Renting Cars/Boats**

For those who prefer not to drive, hiring a car with a driver is an option. Daily hire rates range from NT$3,000 to NT$5,000, depending on the vehicle and itinerary. Private boat charters are available for island hopping and coastal tours. Prices vary widely based on the boat type and duration, but expect to pay around NT$10,000 to NT$20,000 for a day trip.

By utilizing these diverse transportation options, travelers can experience Taiwan's rich culture, natural beauty, and vibrant cities just like a local.

PUBLIC TRANSPORTATION OPTIONS

Taiwan boasts an efficient and comprehensive public transportation system that makes traveling around the island convenient and affordable. Here's everything you need to know about the various options:

- **Taiwan High-Speed Rail (THSR)**

The Taiwan High-Speed Rail is the fastest way to travel between major cities on the west coast. It runs from Taipei in the north to Kaohsiung in the south, with stops in major cities like Taichung and Tainan. The journey from Taipei to Kaohsiung takes about 1.5 to 2 hours. Ticket prices vary by distance and class, with fares from Taipei to Kaohsiung ranging from NT$1,490 for a standard seat to NT$2,440 for a business class seat.

- **Taiwan Railways (TRA)**

The Taiwan Railways Administration operates an extensive network of trains that cover the entire island. There are various types of trains, including the express Puyuma and Taroko, which offer faster travel times. A trip from Taipei to Hualien on the east coast takes about 2 hours and costs around NT$440. TRA trains are a great way to explore smaller towns and scenic areas.

- **Metro Systems**

Taipei and Kaohsiung both have modern metro systems that are efficient and easy to use. The Taipei Metro (MRT) covers the city and its suburbs with extensive lines. Fares range from NT$20 to NT$65, depending on distance. The Kaohsiung MRT is smaller but equally convenient, with fares ranging from NT$20 to NT$60.

- **Buses**

Taiwan's bus network is extensive, covering cities, towns, and rural areas. Long-distance buses connect major cities, with fares from Taipei to Kaohsiung costing around NT$500 to NT$700. City buses in Taipei and other urban areas are frequent and affordable, with single-ride fares typically between NT$15 and NT$30, payable via EasyCard or cash.

- **Taxis**

Taxis are readily available in all major cities and towns. In Taipei, the base fare is NT$70, with additional charges of NT$5 for every 250 meters. Taxi fares are relatively reasonable, but costs can add up for long distances.

- **Bicycles**

Many cities in Taiwan offer bike-sharing programs, such as YouBike in Taipei and Taichung. Renting a YouBike costs NT$10 for the first 30 minutes, making it an affordable and eco-friendly way to explore urban areas.

- **EasyCard and iPASS**

EasyCard and iPASS are rechargeable smart cards that can be used on the metro, buses, and even some taxis and convenience stores. These cards offer discounted fares and convenience, allowing seamless transfers between different modes of public transportation.

- **Ferries**

For travel to outlying islands, ferries are available from major ports like Kaohsiung and Keelung. A ferry ride from Kaohsiung to Penghu takes about 4-5 hours and costs between NT$1,000 and NT$2,000.

By taking advantage of Taiwan's diverse public transportation options, travelers can easily explore the island's vibrant cities, stunning landscapes, and cultural treasures.

CAR RENTALS AND DRIVING TIPS

Renting a car in Taiwan offers flexibility and the freedom to explore the island at your own pace. Here's what you need to know about car rentals and driving like a local:

- CAR RENTALS

- **Airports and Locations**

Car rental services are widely available at major airports, including Taiwan Taoyuan International Airport (TPE), Taipei Songshan Airport (TSA), and Kaohsiung International Airport (KHH). Additionally, you can find rental agencies in city centers and near major train stations.

- **Cost and Booking**

Rental prices start at around NT$1,500 per day for a compact car. Booking in advance online can sometimes secure better rates. Major rental companies include Avis, Hertz, and local brands like Ching Bing and Easy Rent. Insurance is recommended and typically adds NT$300 to NT$500 per day.

- DRIVING TIPS

- **License and Documentation**

International driving permits (IDPs) are accepted in Taiwan, but it's always good to carry your home country's license as well. Ensure your rental agreement and insurance papers are in the vehicle at all times.

- **Road Rules and Signage**

Driving is on the right side of the road. Speed limits are generally 50-60 km/h in cities and 100-110 km/h on highways. Road signs are in both Chinese and English, making navigation easier for international drivers.

- **Fuel and Costs**

Fuel prices in Taiwan are relatively affordable, averaging NT$30 per liter. Gas stations are plentiful, especially along highways and in urban areas.

- MOTORCYCLE AND SCOOTER RENTALS

- **Cost and Requirements**

Scooters are a popular choice for getting around smaller towns and islands. Rental costs range from NT$300 to NT$600 per day. You need a motorcycle license or an IDP with a motorcycle endorsement to rent a scooter.

- **Safety and Helmets**

Wearing a helmet is mandatory, and it's important to drive cautiously, especially in busy urban areas.

- BY BUS

- **Alternative to Renting**

If renting a vehicle is not your preference, Taiwan's bus system is an efficient alternative. Long-distance buses connect major cities, and fares from Taipei to Kaohsiung are around NT$500 to NT$700. City buses are frequent and cost between NT$15 and NT$30.

- BY BOAT

- **Exploring Islands**

For island destinations like Penghu or Green Island, renting a boat or using ferry services is a good option. Private boat rentals vary widely, with prices from

NT$10,000 to NT$20,000 for a day trip, while ferries cost around NT$1,000 to NT$2,000.

- HIRING CARS AND BOATS

- **Chauffeur Services**

For those who prefer not to drive, hiring a car with a driver is available. Rates are approximately NT$3,000 to NT$5,000 per day. Boat charters for coastal tours or island hopping range significantly but start around NT$10,000 for a day.

- **Final Tips**

Always carry cash for tolls and parking fees, which can range from NT$20 to NT$100 per hour in city centers. Be aware of local driving habits, and make sure to park in designated areas to avoid fines.

FOUR

TIME TO VISIT

SEASONAL HIGHLIGHTS

- **Spring (March to May)**

Spring is one of the best times to visit Taiwan. The weather is mild and comfortable, with temperatures ranging from 15°C to 25°C (59°F to 77°F). The island bursts into bloom, with cherry blossoms and other flowers creating picturesque landscapes. One of the most notable events during this season is the Taiwan Lantern Festival, which typically takes place in February or March. Visitors can enjoy intricate lantern displays, fireworks, and traditional performances. Spring is also an excellent time to visit Alishan for the cherry blossom season, offering breathtaking views of blooming sakura against the backdrop of misty mountains.

- **Summer (June to August)**

Summer in Taiwan is hot and humid, with temperatures often exceeding 30°C (86°F). Despite the heat, this season is packed with exciting events and festivals. The Dragon Boat Festival, celebrated in June, features thrilling dragon boat races and festive activities. Beaches along the east coast and in Kenting National Park become popular destinations for sunbathing, swimming, and water sports. Summer is also the season for mangoes, and visitors can savor this tropical fruit at its peak.

- **Autumn (September to November)**

Autumn is another fantastic time to visit Taiwan, with cooler temperatures ranging from 20°C to 28°C (68°F to 82°F). The weather is generally dry and pleasant, making it ideal for outdoor activities. The Mid-Autumn Festival, or Moon Festival, is a significant event celebrated with mooncakes and family gatherings. The Double Ninth Festival, also known as the Senior Citizens Festival, sees families hiking and enjoying chrysanthemum displays. The autumn foliage in places like Yangmingshan National Park and Alishan adds vibrant hues to the already stunning landscapes.

- **Winter (December to February)**

Winter in Taiwan is mild, with temperatures ranging from 10°C to 20°C (50°F to 68°F). This season is perfect for exploring hot springs, particularly in Beitou and Jiaoxi. The Pingxi Sky Lantern Festival, held in February, is a magical event where thousands of lanterns are released into the night sky, creating a mesmerizing spectacle. Winter is also the season for strawberry picking in Miaoli and other rural areas. Although the temperatures are cooler, Taiwan's winter is relatively mild, making it a pleasant escape from harsh winter climates elsewhere.

Taiwan's diverse seasonal highlights ensure there's something special to experience year-round, making it a must-visit destination for any traveler.

EVENTS AND FESTIVALS

- **Taiwan Lantern Festival**

One of the most celebrated events in Taiwan, the Taiwan Lantern Festival usually takes place in February or March. This festival marks the end of the Lunar New Year celebrations. Cities and towns across Taiwan are adorned with beautifully crafted lanterns, each telling a story or showcasing traditional art. The main event is held in a different location each year, featuring grand displays, fireworks, and cultural performances. It's a magical experience to see thousands of lanterns light up the night sky.

- **Dragon Boat Festival**

Held on the fifth day of the fifth lunar month, typically in June, the Dragon Boat Festival is an exciting and culturally rich event. The highlight is the dragon boat races, where teams paddle in sync to the beat of drums, competing for glory on rivers and lakes across Taiwan. Traditional customs include eating zongzi (sticky rice dumplings wrapped in bamboo leaves) and hanging calamus and mugwort on doors to ward off evil spirits.

- **Mid-Autumn Festival**

The Mid-Autumn Festival, or Moon Festival, is celebrated in September or October, during the full moon. Families gather to enjoy mooncakes, a traditional pastry filled with sweet or savory fillings, and to admire the bright, round moon. Public parks and open spaces are filled with people carrying lanterns and enjoying barbecues. It's a time of reunion and reflection, making it a heartwarming festival to witness and participate in.

- **Pingxi Sky Lantern Festival**

The Pingxi Sky Lantern Festival, held in February, is another enchanting event that draws crowds from around the world. Participants write their wishes on lanterns and release them into the sky, creating a stunning visual spectacle as thousands of glowing lanterns float upwards. The festival takes place in the small town of Pingxi, which becomes a hub of activity with food stalls, performances, and the mesmerizing sight of lanterns filling the sky.

- **Taipei International Book Exhibition**

For book lovers, the Taipei International Book Exhibition is a must-visit event, usually held in February. This week-long event features thousands of publishers from around the world, author talks, book signings, and a wide array of literary activities. It's a fantastic opportunity to explore the literary scene and discover new books and authors.

- **Taiwan Pride**

Taiwan Pride, held in October, is the largest LGBTQ+ event in Asia. The vibrant parade through the streets of Taipei celebrates diversity and equality, drawing participants and spectators from around the globe. The event features colorful floats, music, performances, and a joyous atmosphere, reflecting Taiwan's progressive stance on LGBTQ+ rights.

- **New Year's Eve Celebrations**

Taiwan's New Year's Eve celebrations are a grand affair, with Taipei 101 being the focal point. The skyscraper's fireworks display is one of the most spectacular in the world, attracting thousands of spectators. Concerts, parties, and countdown events take place across the island, ensuring a memorable start to the new year.

Attending these festivals and events provides a deeper understanding of Taiwan's rich cultural heritage and vibrant community spirit, making any visit to the island truly unforgettable.

RECOMMENDED DURATION OF STAY

When planning a trip to Taiwan, the duration of your stay plays a crucial role in ensuring you have an enjoyable and fulfilling experience. While Taiwan offers a myriad of attractions and activities, a recommended duration of stay can help you make the most of your visit.

- **Short Stay (3-5 Days)**

A short stay of 3 to 5 days is ideal for first-time visitors who want to get a taste of what Taiwan has to offer. During this period, you can explore the bustling city of Taipei, visit iconic landmarks like Taipei 101, and delve into the rich history at the National Palace Museum. You can also take a day trip to Jiufen, a charming mountain town known for its narrow streets and traditional teahouses. Don't miss the chance to relax in the hot springs of Beitou or enjoy the vibrant night markets such as Shilin and Raohe.

- **Medium Stay (7-10 Days)**

A medium stay of 7 to 10 days allows you to explore Taiwan more thoroughly. Besides Taipei, you can venture to Taichung to see the colorful Rainbow Village and the serene Sun Moon Lake. Spend a couple of days in Tainan, the oldest city in Taiwan, to visit historic temples and enjoy its renowned street food. Head to

Kaohsiung to experience the stunning Fo Guang Shan Buddha Museum and the artistic Pier-2 Art Center. This duration also provides ample time to visit the Taroko Gorge in Hualien, a natural marvel with breathtaking marble canyons and hiking trails.

- **Extended Stay (2 Weeks or More)**

For those with more time, a stay of two weeks or longer offers a comprehensive exploration of Taiwan's diverse landscapes and cultures. You can take a leisurely trip around the island, including visits to Alishan for its famous sunrise views and tea plantations, and Kenting National Park for its beautiful beaches and water activities. Explore the east coast's rugged scenery, including the East Rift Valley and Taitung. You can also discover the indigenous cultures and participate in local festivals. An extended stay allows for a deeper dive into Taiwan's culinary scene, from high-end restaurants to hidden food gems.

- Seasonal Considerations

The best time to visit Taiwan depends on your interests. Spring (March to May) and autumn (September to November) are generally recommended due to pleasant weather. However, each season offers unique experiences, such as summer beach activities or winter hot springs.

Regardless of your duration, Taiwan's efficient transportation system, including high-speed rail and extensive bus networks, makes it easy to get around and explore different regions. Plan your itinerary based on your interests and the time you have, and you're sure to have an unforgettable stay in Taiwan.

FIVE

5-DAY ITINERARY FOR TAIWAN

DAY 1: ARRIVAL AND EXPLORATION OF TAIPEI

- **Morning: Arrival in Taipei**

Arrival at Taiwan Taoyuan International Airport (TPE)

- **Location:** Dayuan District, Taoyuan City, Taiwan
- **Website:** [Taoyuan Airport - https://www.taoyuan-airport.com
- **Distance to Taipei:** Approximately 40 km
- **Taxi Cost:** Around NT$1,000 to NT$1,200 (USD 35-40)
- **Travel Time:** 40-60 minutes

- **Transport to City Center**
- **Airport MRT:** NT$160 (USD 5) to Taipei Main Station, 35 minutes
- **Bus:** NT$125 (USD 4), 55 minutes

- ACCOMMODATION CHECK-IN: RECOMMENDED HOTELS IN TAIPEI

- **The Grand Hotel Taipei**
- **Price per Night:** NT$3,800 (USD 125)
- **Contact:** +886-2-2886-8888

- **Website:** The Grand Hotel - https://www.grand-hotel.org
- **Address:** 1 Zhongshan N Rd, Zhongshan District, Taipei City
- **Amenities:** Pool, fitness center, free Wi-Fi, restaurants
- **Nearby Attractions:** Shilin Night Market, National Palace Museum

- **W Taipei**
- **Price per Night:** NT$7,500 (USD 250)
- **Contact:** +886-2-7703-8888
- **Website:** W Taipei - https://www.marriott.com/hotels/travel/tnwwt-w-taipei/
- **Address:** 10 Zhongxiao East Rd, Xinyi District, Taipei City
- **Amenities:** Pool, spa, fitness center, bars and restaurants
- **Nearby Attractions:** Taipei 101, Sun Yat-sen Memorial Hall

- **Hotel Eclat Taipei**
- **Price per Night:** NT$5,000 (USD 165)
- **Contact:** +886-2-2784-9999
- **Website:** Hotel Eclat - https://www.eclathotels.com/taipei
- **Address:** 370 Section 1, Dunhua South Road, Da'an District, Taipei City
- **Amenities:** Art-themed rooms, free Wi-Fi, breakfast
- **Nearby Attractions:** Da'an Forest Park, Yongkang Street

- **CitizenM Taipei North Gate**
- **Price per Night:** NT$2,800 (USD 95)
- **Contact:** +886-2-2553-6688
- **Website:** CitizenM -
https://www.citizenm.com/destinations/taipei/taipei-north-gate-hotel
- **Address:** 3 Section 1, Zhonghua Road, Zhongzheng District, Taipei City
-**Amenities:** Modern rooms, free Wi-Fi, 24/7 canteenM
- **Nearby Attractions:** Ximending, Taipei Main Station

- **Amba Taipei Ximending**
- **Price per Night:** NT$3,200 (USD 105)
- **Contact:** +886-2-2375-5111
- **Website:** Amba Hotels - https://www.ambahotels.com/en/ximending

- **Address:** 77 Section 2, Wuchang Street, Wanhua District, Taipei City
- **Amenities:** Trendy decor, free Wi-Fi, restaurant
- **Nearby Attractions:** Ximending, Longshan Temple

- **Mid-Morning: Chiang Kai-shek Memorial Hall**
- **Location:** 21 Zhongshan South Road, Zhongzheng District, Taipei City
- **Opening Hours:** 9:00 AM - 6:00 PM
- **Admission:** Free
- **About:** A prominent national monument and landmark, built in memory of the former President of the Republic of China.
- **Top Attractions:** Changing of the guard ceremony (every hour), Liberty Square, National Theater, and National Concert Hall.

- **Lunch: Din Tai Fung**
- **Location:** Basement 1, No. 45, Section 2, Zhongxiao East Road, Da'an District, Taipei City
- **Contact:** +886-2-2321-8928
- **Website:** Din Tai Fung - https://www.dintaifung.com.tw/en/
- **Opening Hours:** 11:00 AM - 9:00 PM
- **Price:** NT$500-800 (USD 16-27) per person
- **Menu:** Famous for xiaolongbao (soup dumplings), steamed buns, and various Taiwanese dishes.

- **Afternoon: Taipei 101**
- **Location:** 7 Section 5, Xinyi Road, Xinyi District, Taipei City
- **Opening Hours:** 9:00 AM - 10:00 PM
- **Admission:** NT$600 (USD 20) for observatory
- **About:** Once the tallest building in the world, Taipei 101 offers breathtaking views of the city from its observatory on the 89th floor.
- **Top Attractions:** Observatory, shopping mall, restaurants.

- **Evening: Shilin Night Market**
- **Location:** No. 101, Jihe Road, Shilin District, Taipei City
- **Opening Hours:** 4:00 PM - 12:00 AM

- **About:** One of the largest and most famous night markets in Taiwan, known for its street food, games, and shops.
- **Top Foods to Try:** Stinky tofu, oyster omelet, fried chicken steak, bubble tea.

- **Outdoor Activities: Elephant Mountain Hiking Trail**

- **Location:** Near Xiangshan MRT Station, Xinyi District, Taipei City
- **Best Time:** Late afternoon for sunset views
- **About:** A popular hiking trail that offers stunning views of Taipei 101 and the city skyline.
- **Pro Tips:** Wear comfortable shoes and bring water. The hike takes about 20-30 minutes.

- **Pro Tips & Don't Miss**

- **Pro Tip:** Start your day early to avoid crowds at popular attractions.
- **Don't Miss:** The changing of the guard at Chiang Kai-shek Memorial Hall, and the sunset view from Elephant Mountain.

This detailed itinerary ensures you experience the best of Taipei on your first day, with insights into key locations, transportation, dining options, and tips to make your visit smooth and memorable.

DAY 2: DISCOVERING TAICHUNG AND SUN MOON LAKE

- MORNING: TRAVELING TO TAICHUNG

- **Transport from Taipei to Taichung**

- **Taiwan High-Speed Rail (THSR):** From Taipei Main Station to Taichung HSR Station
- **Cost:** NT$700-800 (USD 23-27) one way
- **Travel Time:** Approximately 1 hour

- EXPLORING TAICHUNG

- **Rainbow Village**

- **Location:** No. 56, Chun'an Road, Nantun District, Taichung City
- **Opening Hours:** 9:00 AM - 6:00 PM
- **Admission:** Free
- **About:** A colorful and vibrant village painted by a former soldier, Mr. Huang Yung-Fu, also known as the "Rainbow Grandpa."
- **Top Attractions:** Colorful murals and art installations.

- **National Taichung Theater**

- **Location:** No. 101, Section 2, Huilai Road, Xitun District, Taichung City
- **Opening Hours:** 11:30 AM - 9:00 PM
- **Admission:** Free for the building; performances vary in price
- **About:** An architectural marvel designed by Toyo Ito, featuring unique curved walls and stunning acoustics.

- **Top Attractions:** Guided tours, performances, and exhibitions.

- **Lunch: Miyahara**
- **Location:** No. 20, Zhongshan Road, Central District, Taichung City
- **Contact:** +886-4-2227-1927
- **Website:** Miyahara - https://www.dawncake.com.tw/en/
- **Opening Hours:** 10:00 AM - 10:00 PM
- **Price:** NT$300-500 (USD 10-17) per person
- **Menu:** Known for its stunning interior, ice cream, and pastries.

- AFTERNOON: JOURNEY TO SUN MOON LAKE

- **Transport from Taichung to Sun Moon Lake**
- **Bus:** Nantou Bus from Taichung Gancheng Station to Sun Moon Lake
- **Cost:** NT$200-250 (USD 7-8) one way
- **Travel Time:** Approximately 1.5 hours

- **Sun Moon Lake**
- **Location:** Yuchi Township, Nantou County
- **Opening Hours:** 24 hours
- **Admission:** Free; activities and attractions may have fees
- **About:** Taiwan's largest freshwater lake, known for its picturesque scenery and tranquil ambiance.
- **Top Attractions:** Ci'en Pagoda, Wenwu Temple, and the Sun Moon Lake Ropeway.

- **Dinner: The Lalu**
- **Location:** No. 142, Zhongxing Road, Yuchi Township, Nantou County
- **Contact:** +886-49-285-6888
- **Website:** The Lalu - https://www.thelalu.com.tw
- **Opening Hours:** 5:30 PM - 10:00 PM
- **Price:** NT$1,500-2,500 (USD 50-85) per person
- **Menu:** Offers fine dining with a stunning lake view; recommended dishes include local fish and fusion cuisine.

- BEST PLACES TO STAY NEAR SUN MOON LAKE

- **The Lalu**
- **Price per Night:** NT$15,000 (USD 500)
- **Contact:** +886-49-285-6888
- **Website:** The Lalu - https://www.thelalu.com.tw
- **Address:** No. 142, Zhongxing Road, Yuchi Township, Nantou County
- **Amenities:** Infinity pool, spa, lake view rooms
- **Nearby Attractions:** Sun Moon Lake, Wenwu Temple

- **Fleur de Chine Hotel**
- **Price per Night:** NT$10,000 (USD 330)
- **Contact:** +886-49-285-5500
- **Website:** Fleur de Chine - https://www.fleurdechinehotel.com
- **Address:** No. 23, Zhongzheng Road, Yuchi Township, Nantou County
- **Amenities:** Hot springs, pool, lake view
- **Nearby Attractions:** Sun Moon Lake, Ita Thao Village

- **Sun Moon Lake Hotel**
- **Price per Night:** NT$6,000 (USD 200)
- **Contact:** +886-49-285-5111
- **Website:** Sun Moon Lake Hotel - http://www.sunmoonlakehotel.com.tw
- **Address:** No. 419, Zhongshan Road, Yuchi Township, Nantou County
- **Amenities:** Free Wi-Fi, breakfast, bike rentals
- **Nearby Attractions:** Sun Moon Lake, Xiangshan Visitor Center

- **Lealea Garden Hotels - Sun Moon Lake**
- **Price per Night:** NT$4,500 (USD 150)
- **Contact:** +886-49-285-6888
- **Website:** Lealea Garden - https://www.lealeahotel.com.tw
- **Address:** No. 3, Shueishe Village, Yuchi Township, Nantou County
- **Amenities:** Lake view rooms, restaurant, gym
- **Nearby Attractions:** Sun Moon Lake, Shueishe Pier

- **Hotel Del Lago**
- **Price per Night:** NT$5,000 (USD 165)
- **Contact:** +886-49-285-6888
- **Website:** Hotel Del Lago - https://www.hoteldelago.com.tw
- **Address:** No. 101, Zhongshan Road, Yuchi Township, Nantou County
- **Amenities:** Lakefront location, restaurant, free Wi-Fi
- **Nearby Attractions:** Sun Moon Lake, Shueishe Visitor Center

- OUTDOOR ACTIVITIES AT SUN MOON LAKE

- **Boating**
- **Cost:** NT$300 (USD 10) per person for a boat tour
- **Best Time:** Morning or late afternoon

- **Cycling**
- **Cost:** NT$200-300 (USD 7-10) for bike rentals
- **Best Time:** Morning or evening to avoid the heat
- **About:** Scenic cycling path around the lake, offering stunning views.

- **Hiking**
- **Cost:** Free
- **Best Time:** Early morning
- **About:** Trails like the Ci'en Pagoda Trail and the Maolan Mountain Trail offer picturesque views and a peaceful environment.

- **Pro Tips & Don't Miss**
- **Pro Tip:** Purchase a Sun Moon Lake Pass for discounts on transportation and attractions.
- **Don't Miss:** The sunset view from the Ci'en Pagoda and a leisurely boat ride on the lake.

This itinerary ensures a full day of exploration, cultural immersion, and relaxation in Taichung and Sun Moon Lake, complete with travel details, costs, dining options, and top attractions to make your visit unforgettable.

DAY 3: EXPLORING TAINAN AND ANPING OLD FORT

- MORNING: TRAVELING TO TAINAN

- **Transport from Sun Moon Lake to Tainan**

- **Bus and Train:** Take a bus from Sun Moon Lake to Taichung HSR Station, then the Taiwan High-Speed Rail (THSR) to Tainan.

- **Cost:** Approximately NT$900 (USD 30) one way

- **Travel Time:** Approximately 2.5 hours

- EXPLORING TAINAN

- **Anping Old Fort**

- **Location:** No. 82, Guosheng Rd, Anping District, Tainan City

- **Opening Hours:** 8:30 AM - 5:30 PM

- **Admission:** NT$50 (USD 2)

- **About:** Anping Old Fort, also known as Fort Zeelandia, is a historic fort built by the Dutch in the 17th century.

- **Top Attractions:** The old fortifications, museum exhibits, and panoramic views from the watchtower.

- **Anping Tree House**

- **Location:** No. 108, Gubao St, Anping District, Tainan City

- **Opening Hours:** 8:30 AM - 5:30 PM

- **Admission:** NT$70 (USD 2.50)

- **About:** This fascinating site features an old warehouse overgrown with banyan trees, creating a unique and hauntingly beautiful scene.
- **Top Attractions:** The tree-covered structures and nearby exhibits on Tainan's history.

- **Lunch: Chihkan Tower**
- **Location:** No. 212, Section 2, Minzu Rd, West Central District, Tainan City
- **Contact:** +886-6-220-5647
- **Website:** Chihkan Tower - https://www.twtainan.net/en/attractions/detail/4510
- **Opening Hours:** 8:30 AM - 9:30 PM
- **Price:** NT$100-200 (USD 3-7) per person
- **Menu:** Traditional Taiwanese cuisine in a historical setting.

- AFTERNOON: EXPLORING TAINAN'S CULTURAL SITES

- **Chihkan Tower (Fort Provintia)**
- **Location:** No. 212, Section 2, Minzu Rd, West Central District, Tainan City
- **Opening Hours:** 8:30 AM - 9:30 PM
- **Admission:** NT$50 (USD 2)
- **About:** Built by the Dutch in the 17th century, Chihkan Tower is one of Tainan's most iconic historical sites.
- **Top Attractions:** The traditional architecture, historical artifacts, and tranquil gardens.

- **Confucius Temple**
- **Location:** No. 2, Nanmen Rd, West Central District, Tainan City
- **Opening Hours:** 8:30 AM - 5:30 PM
- **Admission:** NT$25 (USD 1)
- **About:** The first Confucius Temple in Taiwan, dating back to 1665, and a beautiful example of classical Chinese architecture.
- **Top Attractions:** The serene courtyards, traditional structures, and cultural exhibits.

- **Dinner: Du Hsiao Yueh**
- **Location:** No. 101, Section 2, Minzu Rd, West Central District, Tainan City

- **Contact:** +886-6-223-1744
- **Website:** Du Hsiao Yueh - https://www.dhsytw.com.tw
- **Opening Hours:** 11:00 AM - 10:00 PM
- **Price:** NT$200-400 (USD 7-14) per person
- **Menu:** Famous for its danzai noodles and traditional Taiwanese dishes.

- BEST PLACES TO STAY IN TAINAN

- **Shangri-La's Far Eastern Plaza Hotel**

- **Price per Night:** NT$4,500 (USD 150)
- **Contact:** +886-6-702-8888
- **Website:** Shangri-La Tainan -
https://www.shangri-la.com/tainan/fareasternplazashangrila/
- **Address:** No. 89, Section West, University Road, East District, Tainan City
- **Amenities:** Pool, gym, spa, restaurants
- **Nearby Attractions:** Tainan Confucius Temple, Tainan Art Museum

- **Silks Place Tainan**

- **Price per Night:** NT$4,000 (USD 135)
- **Contact:** +886-6-213-6290
- **Website:** Silks Place - https://www.silksplace-tainan.com
- **Address:** No. 1, Heyi Rd, West Central District, Tainan City
- **Amenities:** Rooftop pool, fitness center, restaurant
- **Nearby Attractions:** Chihkan Tower, Tainan Wu Garden

- **Taipung Suites**

- **Price per Night:** NT$2,800 (USD 95)
- **Contact:** +886-6-213-5555
- **Website:** Taipung Suites - https://www.taipungsuites.com.tw
- **Address:** No. 199, Yonghua 2nd St, Anping District, Tainan City
- **Amenities:** Free breakfast, fitness center, free parking
- **Nearby Attractions:** Anping Old Fort, Tainan City Hall

- **U.I.J Hotel & Hostel**
- **Price per Night:** NT$2,000 (USD 70)
- **Contact:** +886-6-221-8188
- **Website:** U.I.J Hotel - https://www.uijhotel.com
- **Address:** No. 5, Ln. 115, You'ai St, West Central District, Tainan City
- **Amenities:** Library, café, free Wi-Fi
- **Nearby Attractions:** Tainan Art Museum, Shennong Street

- **Jack House**
- **Price per Night:** NT$1,500 (USD 50)
- **Contact:** +886-6-221-5118
- **Website:** Jack House - https://www.jackhouse.com
- **Address:** No. 10, Lane 141, Section 2, Minzu Rd, West Central District, Tainan City
- **Amenities:** Free breakfast, bicycle rental, common area
- **Nearby Attractions:** Chihkan Tower, Tainan Wu Garden

- OUTDOOR ACTIVITIES IN TAINAN

- **Anping Canal Tour**
- **Cost:** NT$200 (USD 7) per person
- **Best Time:** Late afternoon to evening
- **About:** A leisurely boat tour along the historic Anping Canal.

- **Biking along Anping District**
- **Cost:** NT$100-200 (USD 3-7) for bike rentals
- **Best Time:** Morning or late afternoon
- **About:** Explore Anping's scenic bike paths and historic sites.

- **Walking Tour of Historical Sites**
- **Cost:** Free
- **Best Time:** Early morning or late afternoon

- **About:** A self-guided walking tour of Tainan's many historical and cultural landmarks.

- • **Pro Tips & Don't Miss**
- **Pro Tip:** Wear comfortable shoes for walking and exploring the historical sites.
- **Don't Miss:** The sunset view from Anping Old Fort and the evening canal tour.

This itinerary ensures a full day of cultural immersion, historical exploration, and relaxation in Tainan, complete with travel details, costs, dining options, and top attractions to make your visit unforgettable.

DAY 4: RELAXING DAY IN KENTING NATIONAL PARK

- MORNING: TRAVELING TO KENTING NATIONAL PARK

- • **Transport from Tainan to Kenting**
- **Bus:** Take the Kuo-Kuang or Pingtung Bus from Tainan to Kenting.
- **Cost:** Approximately NT$500 (USD 17) one way.
- **Travel Time:** Approximately 3 hours.

- EXPLORING KENTING NATIONAL PARK

- • **Kenting National Park**
- **Location:** Hengchun Peninsula, Pingtung County.
- **Opening Hours:** Open 24 hours.
- **Admission:** Free.

- **About:** Kenting National Park is Taiwan's oldest and most famous national park, known for its tropical climate, beautiful beaches, and diverse ecosystems.
- **Top Attractions:** Eluanbi Lighthouse, Maobitou Park, and the Longpan Park cliffs.

- OUTDOOR ACTIVITIES IN KENTING NATIONAL PARK

- **Snorkeling at Baisha Beach**
- **Cost:** NT$300-500 (USD 10-17) for gear rental.
- **Best Time:** Morning to early afternoon.
- **About:** Baisha Beach is known for its clear waters and excellent snorkeling opportunities.

- **Hiking in Kenting National Forest Recreation Area**
- **Cost:** NT$150 (USD 5) for entry.
- **Best Time:** Early morning or late afternoon.
- **About:** A beautiful area with hiking trails, botanical gardens, and diverse wildlife.

- LUNCH: LOCAL CUISINE IN KENTING

- **Smokey Joe's**
- **Location:** No. 237, Kending Rd, Hengchun Township, Pingtung County.
- **Contact:** +886-8-886-2323
- **Website:** Smokey Joe's - http://www.smokeyjoesgroup.com/
- **Opening Hours:** 11:00 AM - 10:00 PM
- **Price:** NT$300-600 (USD 10-20) per person.
- **Menu:** A mix of Mexican and American cuisine with a tropical twist.
- **Pro Tip:** Try their famous ribs and margaritas.

- AFTERNOON: EXPLORING MORE OF KENTING

- **Eluanbi Lighthouse**
- **Location:** No. 90, Eluan Rd, Hengchun Township, Pingtung County.
- **Opening Hours:** 7:00 AM - 6:00 PM
- **Admission:** NT$60 (USD 2)

- **About:** Known as the "Light of East Asia," it's one of the most prominent lighthouses in Taiwan.
- **Top Attractions:** The lighthouse itself, the surrounding park, and the stunning coastal views.

- **Maobitou Park**

- **Location:** No. 1-5, Daguang Rd, Hengchun Township, Pingtung County.
- **Opening Hours:** 24 hours.
- **Admission:** Free.
- **About:** Offers dramatic views of the coastline and unique rock formations.
- **Top Attractions:** Panoramic sea views and the famous "Cat's Nose" rock formation.

- DINNER: SEAFOOD BY THE COAST

- **Kenting Night Market**

- Location: Kenting Road, Hengchun Township, Pingtung County.
- Opening Hours: 6:00 PM - 12:00 AM
- Price: NT$200-400 (USD 7-14) per person.
- Menu: Street food including fresh seafood, BBQ, and local delicacies.
- Pro Tip: Don't miss trying the grilled squid and mango shaved ice.

- BEST PLACES TO STAY IN KENTING

- **Caesar Park Hotel Kenting**

- **Price per Night:** NT$7,000 (USD 235)
- **Contact:** +886-8-886-1888
- **Website:** Caesar Park Kenting - https://www.caesarpark.com.tw/
- **Address:** No. 6, Kenting Rd, Hengchun Township, Pingtung County.
- **Amenities:** Private beach, pool, spa, and multiple dining options.
- **Nearby Attractions:** Kenting Street, Eluanbi Park.

- **Howard Beach Resort Kenting**

- **Price per Night:** NT$5,500 (USD 185)

- **Contact:** +886-8-886-2323
- **Website:** Howard Beach Resort - https://www.howard-hotels.com.tw/
- **Address:** No. 2, Kenting Rd, Hengchun Township, Pingtung County.
- **Amenities:** Pool, fitness center, kids' club.
- **Nearby Attractions:** Little Bay Beach, Kenting Street.

- **Kenting Amanda Hotel**
- **Price per Night:** NT$3,800 (USD 130)
- **Contact:** +886-8-888-3399
- **Website:** Amanda Hotel - https://www.amanda-hotel.com.tw/
- **Address:** No. 330, Nanwan Rd, Hengchun Township, Pingtung County.
- **Amenities:** Moroccan-themed decor, pool, free breakfast.
- **Nearby Attractions:** Nanwan Beach, Kenting National Park.

- **The Richforest Hotel - Kenting**
- **Price per Night:** NT$4,200 (USD 140)
- **Contact:** +886-8-886-2345
- **Website:** The Richforest - http://www.richforest.com.tw/
- **Address:** No. 137, Kenting Rd, Hengchun Township, Pingtung County.
- **Amenities:** Pool, restaurant, free Wi-Fi.
- **Nearby Attractions:** Kenting National Park, Chuhuo Special Scenic Area.

- **The Riverside Hotel Hengchun**
- **Price per Night:** NT$2,500 (USD 85)
- **Contact:** +886-8-888-2211
- **Website:** Riverside Hotel - https://www.riverside.com.tw/
- **Address:** No. 123, Hengnan Rd, Hengchun Township, Pingtung County.
- **Amenities:** Free breakfast, bike rental, family rooms.
- **Nearby Attractions:** Hengchun Old Town, Kenting Night Market.

- **Pro Tips & Don't Miss**
- **Pro Tip:** Bring sunscreen, a hat, and plenty of water to stay hydrated.
- **Don't Miss:** The sunset at Maobitou Park and the vibrant atmosphere of Kenting Night Market.

This itinerary ensures a relaxed yet adventurous day in Kenting National Park, filled with natural beauty, cultural sites, and culinary delights.

DAY 5: DEPARTURE AND FAREWELL TO TAIWAN

- MORNING: LAST DAY IN TAIPEI

- **Breakfast at Fuhang Soy Milk**

- **Location:** 2nd Floor, No. 108, Section 1, Zhongxiao East Road, Zhongzheng District, Taipei City.

- **Contact:** +886-2-2392-2175

- **Opening Hours:** 5:30 AM - 12:30 PM

- **Price:** NT$50-150 (USD 2-5) per person.

- **Menu:** Traditional Taiwanese breakfast including soy milk, youtiao (fried dough sticks), and dan bing (egg crepes).

- **Pro Tip:** Arrive early to avoid long lines.

- MORNING ACTIVITY: VISIT CHIANG KAI-SHEK MEMORIAL HALL

- **Chiang Kai-Shek Memorial Hall**

- **Location:** No. 21, Zhongshan South Road, Zhongzheng District, Taipei City.

- **Opening Hours:** 9:00 AM - 6:00 PM

- **Admission:** Free.

- **About:** A national monument and tourist attraction, this hall commemorates the former President of the Republic of China, Chiang Kai-Shek.

- **Top Attractions:** The grand hall, the changing of the guard, and the surrounding Liberty Square.

- **Cost:** Free.

- LUNCH: DINE AT DIN TAI FUNG

- **Din Tai Fung**

- **Location:** No. 194, Section 2, Xinyi Road, Da'an District, Taipei City.
- **Contact:** +886-2-2321-8928
- **Opening Hours:** 10:00 AM - 9:00 PM
- **Price:** NT$300-600 (USD 10-20) per person.
- **Menu:** Famous for their xiao long bao (soup dumplings), along with other Taiwanese and Chinese dishes.
- **Pro Tip:** Make a reservation to avoid a long wait.

- AFTERNOON: LAST-MINUTE SHOPPING AT XIMENDING

- **Ximending Shopping District**

- **Location:** Wanhua District, Taipei City.
- **Opening Hours:** Varies by store, generally 11:00 AM - 10:00 PM
- **About:** Known as the "Harajuku of Taipei," Ximending is a bustling shopping area with trendy boutiques, street food, and entertainment.
- **Top Attractions:** Red House Theater, Eslite Bookstore, and various street performances.
- **Cost:** Varies depending on purchases.

- LATE AFTERNOON: RETURN TO HOTEL AND PREPARE FOR DEPARTURE

- **Packing and Hotel Check-Out**

- **Cost:** Ensure no additional charges for late check-out, typically free until 12:00 PM, late check-out may incur a fee.

- DINNER: FINAL MEAL AT SHILIN NIGHT MARKET

- **Shilin Night Market**

- **Location:** No. 101, Jihe Road, Shilin District, Taipei City.
- **Opening Hours:** 4:00 PM - 12:00 AM

- **Price:** NT$200-400 (USD 7-14) per person.
- **Menu:** A variety of street foods including stinky tofu, oyster omelets, bubble tea, and more.
- **Pro Tip:** Arrive early for easier navigation and to avoid the peak crowd.

- EVENING: DEPARTURE FROM TAIWAN

- **Taiwan Taoyuan International Airport**
- **Location:** No. 9, Hangzhan South Road, Dayuan District, Taoyuan City.
- **Distance from Taipei:** Approximately 40 km.
- **Taxi Cost:** NT$1,000-1,200 (USD 35-40)
- **Travel Time:** Approximately 45 minutes.
- **Website:** Taiwan Taoyuan International Airport - https://www.taoyuan-airport.com/
- **About:** The main international airport serving Taipei and northern Taiwan, offering a range of facilities including shopping, dining, and relaxation lounges.

- TOP HOTELS IN TAIPEI

- The Grand Hotel
- **Price per Night:** NT$5,000 (USD 165)
- **Contact:** +886-2-2886-8888
- **Website:** The Grand Hotel - https://www.grand-hotel.org/
- **Address:** No. 1, Section 4, Zhongshan North Road, Zhongshan District, Taipei City.
- **Amenities:** Pool, fitness center, multiple dining options.
- **Nearby Attractions:** Shilin Night Market, National Palace Museum.

- **W Taipei**
- **Price per Night:** NT$10,000 (USD 330)
- **Contact:** +886-2-7703-8888
- **Website:** W Taipei - https://www.marriott.com/hotels/travel/tpewh-w-taipei/
- **Address:** No. 10, Section 5, Zhongxiao East Road, Xinyi District, Taipei City.
- **Amenities:** Rooftop pool, spa, trendy bars and restaurants.
- **Nearby Attractions:** Taipei 101, Sun Yat-sen Memorial Hall.

- **Hotel Proverbs Taipei**
- **Price per Night:** NT$7,000 (USD 230)
- **Contact:** +886-2-2711-1118
- **Website:** Hotel Proverbs Taipei - https://www.hotelproverbs.com/
- **Address:** No. 56, Section 1, Da'an Road, Da'an District, Taipei City.
- **Amenities:** Rooftop pool, Michelin-starred restaurant, chic design.
- **Nearby Attractions:** Yongkang Street, Daan Forest Park.

- **Kimpton Da An Taipei**
- **Price per Night:** NT$6,000 (USD 200)
- **Contact:** +886-2-2713-6600
- **Website:** Kimpton Da An Taipei - https://www.ihg.com/kimptonhotels/hotels/us/en/taipei/tsakd/hoteldetail
- **Address:** No. 25, Lane 27, Section 4, Zhongxiao East Road, Da'an District, Taipei City.
- **Amenities:** Fitness center, complimentary evening social hour.
- **Nearby Attractions:** Breeze Center, Daan Park.

- **Amba Taipei Ximending**
- **Price per Night:** NT$3,500 (USD 115)
- **Contact:** +886-2-2375-5111
- **Website:** Amba Taipei Ximending - https://www.amba-hotels.com/en/ximending/
- **Address:** No. 77, Section 2, Wuchang Street, Wanhua District, Taipei City.
- **Amenities:** Hip, modern design, restaurant, and bar.
- **Nearby Attractions:** Ximending Shopping District, Red House Theater.

- **Pro Tips & Don't Miss**
- **Pro Tip:** Ensure to have sufficient cash in NT$ for last-minute expenses and taxi fare.
- **Don't Miss:** A final stroll through Ximending or a visit to the iconic Taipei 101 for a last view of the city.

This itinerary ensures a smooth and enjoyable final day in Taiwan, highlighting last-minute shopping, cultural sites, and dining experiences before a comfortable departure.

SIX

MUST-SEE DESTINATIONS

TAIPEI 101

- **Historical Background**

Taipei 101, once the tallest building in the world, is an architectural marvel and a symbol of Taiwan's rapid development and technological prowess. Completed in 2004, it was designed by the architect C.Y. Lee and Partners to resemble a bamboo stalk, a symbol of growth and strength in Chinese culture. This skyscraper stood as the tallest building globally until 2010, when it was surpassed by the Burj Khalifa in Dubai. Taipei 101 remains a testament to Taiwan's ambition and innovation.

- **Opening Hours & Admission Fees**
- **Opening Hours:** 9:00 AM - 10:00 PM daily.
- **Admission Fees: Observation Deck** - NT$600 (USD 20) for adults; NT$540 (USD 18) for seniors (65+) and children (6-12 years).
- **Shopping and Dining:** Free entry, but purchases vary.
- **Address:** No. 7, Section 5, Xinyi Road, Xinyi District, Taipei City, 11049, Taiwan.
- **Contact:** +886-2-8101-8800
- **Website:** [Taipei 101 - https://www.taipei-101.com.tw/en/)

- **Getting There**

Taipei 101 is centrally located in the Xinyi District, a bustling area known for its modernity and shopping. To reach Taipei 101:

- **By MRT:** Take the Taipei MRT to the Taipei 101/World Trade Center Station (Blue Line). The building is directly connected to the MRT station via an underground walkway.

- **By Taxi:** Easily accessible by taxi from any part of Taipei. The fare is approximately NT$200-300 (USD 7-10) from Taipei Main Station.

- **By Bus:** Multiple bus routes pass by Taipei 101, with several stops conveniently located around the building.

- **Why Tourists Visit**

Tourists flock to Taipei 101 for its breathtaking views from the observation deck, which offers a panoramic view of Taipei City and beyond. The building also houses a high-end shopping mall and a diverse range of dining options. The highlight is the massive, state-of-the-art tuned mass damper, which stabilizes the building against typhoons and earthquakes, symbolizing Taiwan's resilience.

- **Outdoor Activities**

While Taipei 101 itself is mostly an indoor attraction, visitors can enjoy a stroll in the nearby Taipei 101 Park, which provides a pleasant green space and scenic views of the skyscraper. Additionally, the area around Taipei 101 is excellent for shopping and dining.

- **Pro Tips & Don't Miss**

- **Pro Tip:** Visit the observation deck on a clear day for the best views. Consider going early in the morning or late in the afternoon to avoid crowds and enjoy the sunset.

- **Don't Miss:** The "Taipei 101 Green" rooftop garden, accessible from the observation deck, offers a unique view of the city and a refreshing outdoor experience. Also, explore the lower floors for exclusive shopping and dining options.

Taipei 101 is not just a skyscraper but a centerpiece of Taipei's skyline, blending modern engineering with cultural symbolism.

SUN MOON LAKE

- **Historical Background**

Sun Moon Lake, located in central Taiwan's Nantou County, is renowned for its breathtaking beauty and rich cultural heritage. This picturesque lake has been a significant site for centuries, revered by the Thao people, one of Taiwan's indigenous tribes. Its name derives from its unique shape; the eastern side of the lake resembles a crescent moon, while the western side looks like a sun. This natural wonder has been celebrated in Taiwanese literature and art and continues to be a symbol of Taiwan's natural splendor.

- **Opening Hours & Admission Fees**

- **Opening Hours:** The lake is accessible year-round, 24 hours a day. However, the surrounding facilities such as the visitor centers and boat services operate typically from 8:00 AM to 5:00 PM.
- **Admission Fees: Boat Tour** - NT$300-500 (USD 10-17) depending on the type and duration of the tour.
- **Visitor Centers:** Generally free to enter, but some attractions may have small fees.
- **Address:** No. 5, Wenhua Road, Nantou City, Nantou County, 555, Taiwan.
- **Contact:** +886-49-285-5355
- **Website:** Sun Moon Lake - http://www.sunmoonlake.gov.tw/

- **Getting There**

Sun Moon Lake is located approximately 200 kilometers (124 miles) from Taipei, and there are several ways to reach it:

- **By Bus:** Direct buses to Sun Moon Lake are available from Taipei Main Station and Taichung Railway Station, with travel times of around 2.5 to 3 hours.
- **By Train:** Take the train to Taichung Station, then transfer to a local bus or taxi to reach Sun Moon Lake, which takes approximately 1.5 hours.
- **By Car:** Renting a car is a convenient option. The drive from Taipei takes about 2.5 hours.

- **Why Tourists Visit**

Sun Moon Lake is famed for its serene beauty, surrounded by lush mountains and clear blue waters. It's a popular destination for its scenic boat rides, picturesque walking trails, and cultural landmarks such as the Wenwu Temple and the Formosan Aboriginal Culture Village. The lake also offers a tranquil escape from the hustle and bustle of city life.

- **Outdoor Activities**

Visitors can enjoy a variety of outdoor activities including:
- **Boat Tours:** Scenic rides around the lake, offering stunning views of the surrounding landscape.
- **Cycling:** Rent a bike to explore the lakeside trails and enjoy the natural beauty.
- **Hiking:** Trails like the Ci'en Pagoda offer panoramic views of the lake and its surroundings.

- **Pro Tips & Don't Miss**

- **Pro Tip:** Visit early in the morning or late in the afternoon to avoid crowds and capture the lake's most beautiful lighting.
- **Don't Miss:** The iconic Wenwu Temple, perched on the northern shore, offers spectacular views and rich cultural heritage. Also, don't miss the chance to sample local tea, which is renowned for its quality and flavor.

Sun Moon Lake's combination of natural beauty and cultural significance makes it an essential stop for anyone traveling to Taiwan.

TAROKO GORGE

- **Historical Background**

Taroko Gorge, often hailed as one of Taiwan's most spectacular natural wonders, is located in Taroko National Park, Hualien County. Formed millions of years ago through the relentless force of the Liwu River carving through marble rock, the gorge is renowned for its dramatic landscapes and geological features. The name "Taroko" is derived from the Atayal indigenous word for "magnificent and beautiful." The area has been an important cultural site for the indigenous Truku people, who have lived in harmony with the landscape for centuries.

- **Opening Hours & Admission Fees**

- **Opening Hours:** The gorge and its main attractions are open year-round. Visitor centers typically operate from 8:00 AM to 5:00 PM.

- **Admission Fees:** Entry to Taroko National Park is free. However, some attractions and activities within the park may require additional fees, such as guided tours or bike rentals.

- **Address:** Taroko National Park Headquarters, No. 91, Pingjiang Road, Xiulin Township, Hualien County, 972, Taiwan.

- **Contact:** +886-3-869-2321

- **Website:** Taroko National Park - http://www.taroko.gov.tw/

- **Getting There**

Taroko Gorge is accessible from Hualien City, approximately 30 kilometers (19 miles) away:

- **By Bus:** Regular buses operate between Hualien Train Station and Taroko Gorge. The journey takes about 40 minutes.
- **By Train:** Take the train to Hualien Station, then transfer to a local bus or taxi to reach the gorge.
- **By Car:** Renting a car is a convenient option, with a drive from Hualien City taking around 40 minutes. The park has ample parking areas.

- **Why Tourists Visit**

Taroko Gorge is famous for its breathtaking scenery, including towering marble cliffs, lush forests, and the crystal-clear Liwu River. Visitors come to marvel at natural wonders such as the Eternal Spring Shrine and the Swallow Grotto, which offer spectacular views and photographic opportunities. The gorge is a popular destination for nature lovers and adventure enthusiasts alike.

- **Outdoor Activities**

Visitors can engage in a range of outdoor activities:

- **Hiking:** Trails like the Shakadang Trail and the Baiyang Trail offer stunning views and varying difficulty levels.
- **Cycling:** Rent a bike to explore the gorge and its scenic paths.
- **Photography:** Capture the dramatic landscapes and unique geological formations.

- **Pro Tips & Don't Miss**

- **Pro Tip:** Wear comfortable walking shoes and bring rain gear, as weather conditions can change rapidly. Also, check trail conditions before setting out.
- **Don't Miss:** The Tunnel of Nine Turns for its awe-inspiring views and the beautiful marble formations of the Swallow Grotto. Additionally, take the time to visit the Eternal Spring Shrine, a picturesque spot dedicated to workers who lost their lives during the construction of the Central Cross-Island Highway.

Taroko Gorge's stunning natural beauty and rich cultural heritage make it a must-see destination for anyone visiting Taiwan.

NATIONAL PALACE MUSEUM

- **Historical Background**

The National Palace Museum, located in Taipei, is home to one of the world's most extensive collections of Chinese imperial artifacts. Its origins trace back to the early 20th century when the collection was moved from Beijing to Taiwan during the Chinese Civil War. The museum was established in 1965 to house these treasures, which include ancient Chinese ceramics, jade, calligraphy, and paintings. The museum's mission is to preserve and exhibit China's cultural heritage, making it a key institution in understanding Chinese history and art.

- **Opening Hours & Admission Fees**

- **Opening Hours:** The museum is open daily from 8:30 AM to 6:30 PM, with extended hours until 9:00 PM on Fridays and Saturdays.

- **Admission Fees: Adults** - NT$350 (USD 11)

- **Students and Seniors:** NT$150 (USD 5)

- **Children under 12:** Free

- **Address:** No. 221, Sec 2, Zhi Shan Road, Shih Lin District, Taipei City, 11143, Taiwan.

- **Contact:** +886-2-2881-2021

- **Website:** National Palace Museum - http://www.npm.gov.tw/

- **Getting There**

The National Palace Museum is easily accessible from various parts of Taipei:

- **By MRT:** Take the Taipei MRT Red Line to Shilin Station, then transfer to Bus R30, which will take you directly to the museum. The journey takes about 15 minutes from Shilin Station.

- **By Bus:** Several city buses (e.g., Bus 255) provide direct routes to the museum from different areas of Taipei.
- **By Taxi:** A taxi ride from Taipei Main Station to the museum takes approximately 20 minutes.

- **Why Tourists Visit**

The museum is renowned for its vast collection of over 600,000 pieces of Chinese art, including the famous Jade Cabbage and the Meat-shaped Stone. Visitors come to marvel at these priceless artifacts, which offer insight into the richness of Chinese history and culture. The museum's exhibitions are meticulously curated, making it a premier destination for history and art enthusiasts.

- **Outdoor Activities**

While the museum primarily focuses on indoor exhibits, the surrounding Shih Lin District offers lovely parks and gardens for leisurely walks. The nearby Shilin Night Market is also a popular spot for sampling local Taiwanese street food.

- **Pro Tips & Don't Miss**

- **Pro Tip:** Avoid peak hours and weekends if possible to enjoy a quieter experience. Consider joining a guided tour for deeper insights into the exhibits.
- **Don't Miss:** The Jade Cabbage and the Meat-shaped Stone are must-see highlights. Also, visit the museum's beautiful outdoor gardens for a relaxing stroll and scenic views of Taipei.

The National Palace Museum's impressive collection and rich history make it an essential stop for anyone exploring Taiwan's cultural heritage.

ALISHAN NATIONAL SCENIC AREA

- **Historical Background**

Alishan National Scenic Area, located in Chiayi County, is renowned for its stunning natural beauty and cultural significance. This high-altitude region has been a beloved destination for both locals and tourists for over a century. The area gained prominence during the Japanese colonial period when it was developed as a logging site, and later, as a tourist destination. Today, it's famous for its ancient cypress trees, majestic mountain scenery, and the Alishan Forest Railway, which dates back to the early 20th century and was initially built to transport timber.

- **Opening Hours & Admission Fees**

- **Opening Hours:** The scenic area is open daily from 6:00 AM to 6:00 PM. The Alishan Forest Railway operates from early morning until late afternoon.
- **Admission Fees: Entrance -** NT$150 (USD 5) for adults.
- **Alishan Forest Railway:** NT$400 (USD 13) for a round trip.
- **Address:** Alishan Township, Chiayi County, 604, Taiwan.
- **Contact:** +886-5-259-2170
- **Website:** Alishan National Scenic Area - http://www.ali-shan.com.tw/

- **Getting There**

- **By Train:** Take the Taiwan High-Speed Rail (THSR) to Chiayi Station, then transfer to the Alishan Forest Railway at the Chiayi Railway Station. The train journey to Alishan takes about 2 hours.
- **By Bus:** Several bus services operate from Chiayi City to Alishan, taking approximately 2.5 hours.

- **By Car:** Renting a car is a convenient option. The drive from Chiayi City to Alishan takes around 1.5 to 2 hours, with parking available at the entrance.

- **Why Tourists Visit**

Alishan is renowned for its breathtaking sunrise views over the sea of clouds, lush forests, and scenic mountain trails. Visitors are drawn to its beautiful hiking paths, ancient cedar trees, and the enchanting Alishan Forest Railway, which provides a picturesque ride through the mountains.

- **Outdoor Activities**

- **Hiking:** Popular trails include the Sisters Ponds Trail and the Shouzhen Temple Trail.

- **Sunrise Viewing:** The best spots to watch the sunrise are the viewing platforms near the Alishan Train Station.

- **Cypress Forest Walks:** Explore the ancient cypress trees and serene forest paths.

- **Pro Tips & Don't Miss**

- **Pro Tip:** Bring warm clothing, as temperatures can drop significantly in the early morning and late evening. Also, check the weather forecast before planning your sunrise trip.

- **Don't Miss:** The iconic sunrise view from the Alishan Sunrise Viewing Area and a ride on the historic Alishan Forest Railway. The Sacred Tree and the Three Sisters Ponds are also must-see attractions.

Alishan National Scenic Area's natural beauty and rich cultural heritage make it a quintessential destination for any traveler exploring Taiwan.

SEVEN

DISCOVERING THE CULTURAL CAPITAL

EXPLORING TAIPEI

- **Historical Background**

Taipei, the vibrant capital of Taiwan, is a city where the past and present blend seamlessly. Founded in the 18th century, Taipei grew rapidly during the Japanese colonial period (1895-1945) and has since evolved into a modern metropolis while preserving its rich heritage. Historically, Taipei was a center for trade and culture, reflecting a unique mix of traditional Chinese influences and Japanese modernization. Today, it is renowned for its dynamic culture, historical landmarks, and bustling urban life.

- **Opening Hours & Admission Fees**

- **Taipei 101 Observatory:** Open daily from 9:00 AM to 10:00 PM, with admission fees of NT$600 (USD 20) for adults and NT$540 (USD 18) for children and seniors.

- **National Palace Museum:** Open daily from 8:30 AM to 6:30 PM (extended hours on Fridays and Saturdays until 9:00 PM). Admission is NT$350 (USD 11) for adults, NT$150 (USD 5) for students and seniors, and free for children under 12.

- **Chiang Kai-shek Memorial Hall:** Open daily from 9:00 AM to 6:00 PM, with free admission.

- **Address & Contact Information**

- **Taipei 101:** No. 7, Section 5, Xinyi Road, Taipei City, 11049, Taiwan. - **Contact:** +886-2-8101-8822. - **Website :** https://www.taipei101.com.tw/
- **National Palace Museum:** No. 221, Section 2, Zhi Shan Road, Shih Lin District, Taipei City, 11143, Taiwan. - **Contact:** +886-2-2881-2021. - **Website :** http://www.npm.gov.tw/
- **Chiang Kai-shek Memorial Hall:** No. 21, Zhongshan South Road, Zhongzheng District, Taipei City, 100, Taiwan. - **Contact:** +886-2-2343-1100. - **Website :** https://www.cksmh.gov.tw/

- **Getting There**
- **By MRT:** Taipei's efficient MRT system connects key attractions. Taipei 101 is accessible via the Taipei 101/World Trade Center Station (Red Line), while the National Palace Museum is reachable from Shilin Station (Red Line) with a short bus ride.
- **By Bus:** Buses throughout Taipei also connect major landmarks. The Taipei 101 area is served by several city buses.
- **By Taxi:** Taxis are readily available and a convenient option for traveling between attractions.

- **Why Tourists Visit**
Taipei is a must-visit for its rich cultural tapestry. Tourists flock to Taipei 101 for panoramic views, explore the National Palace Museum for historical artifacts, and visit Chiang Kai-shek Memorial Hall for a glimpse into Taiwan's political history. The city's night markets, such as Shilin and Raohe, offer a taste of local cuisine and vibrant street life.

- **Outdoor Activities**
- **Taipei 101 Observatory:** Enjoy breathtaking city views.
- **Chiang Kai-shek Memorial Hall:** Explore the expansive gardens and historical exhibits.
- **Taipei's Night Markets:** Experience bustling street food culture and local shopping.

- **Pro Tips & Don't Miss**

- **Pro Tip:** Purchase a Taipei Pass for unlimited MRT rides and discounts at various attractions. Visit popular spots early to avoid crowds and enjoy a more leisurely experience.
- **Don't Miss:** The view from Taipei 101's observatory, the intricate exhibits at the National Palace Museum, and the ceremonial changing of the guard at Chiang Kai-shek Memorial Hall. Also, take time to explore Taipei's vibrant night markets for an authentic taste of local life.

Exploring Taipei offers a rich tapestry of cultural, historical, and modern experiences, making it a key destination for anyone visiting Taiwan.

SHOPPING AND DINING EXPERIENCES

Taipei, a dynamic city blending modernity with tradition, offers an array of shopping and dining experiences that captivate every visitor. Here's a guide to the top shopping districts and dining spots in Taipei.

- **Ximending**

Often referred to as Taipei's "Harajuku," Ximending is a bustling shopping district known for its vibrant street fashion, trendy boutiques, and youthful energy. Located in the Wanhua District, Ximending is easily accessible via the Ximen MRT Station (Exit 6). The area is renowned for its eclectic mix of international brands, local designers, and quirky shops. **Opening Hours:** Shops generally open from 11:00 AM to 10:00 PM. **Admission:** Free. Visitors should explore the pedestrianized streets and vibrant night market for unique fashion finds and local accessories.

- **Taipei 101 Mall**

Situated within the iconic Taipei 101 building, Taipei 101 Mall offers a luxury shopping experience with high-end brands like Gucci, Louis Vuitton, and Prada. Located in the Xinyi District, it is easily reachable via Taipei 101/World Trade Center MRT Station. **Opening Hours:** Daily from 11:00 AM to 9:00 PM. **Admission:** Free. The mall is a must-visit for high fashion and luxury goods, providing a panoramic view of the city from the observatory on the upper floors.

- **Zhongxiao Dunhua**

Zhongxiao Dunhua is a premier shopping and dining district in Taipei, known for its chic boutiques and upscale lifestyle stores. This area, located in the Zhongshan District, is accessible via Zhongxiao Dunhua MRT Station (Exit 1). **Opening Hours:** Shops and eateries typically open from 11:00 AM to 10:00 PM. **Admission:** Free. The district offers a blend of designer stores, trendy cafes, and specialty shops, perfect for both shopping and a leisurely meal.

- **Shilin Night Market**

For a more traditional shopping and dining experience, Shilin Night Market is the place to be. Located in the Shilin District, it is accessible via the Jiantan MRT Station. **Opening Hours:** Daily from 4:00 PM to midnight. **Admission:** Free. Known for its vibrant atmosphere, the market offers a variety of street foods, local snacks, and souvenirs. Don't miss out on Taiwanese delicacies like stinky tofu, bubble tea, and fried chicken.

- **Raohe Street Night Market**

Another popular night market is Raohe Street Night Market, located in the Songshan District near the Raohe Street MRT Station. **Opening Hours:** Daily from 5:00 PM to midnight. **Admission:** Free. This market is famed for its authentic street food, including pepper buns, grilled seafood, and traditional pastries. It's also a great spot to pick up unique gifts and local crafts.

- **Pro Tips & What to Look Out For**

- **Pro Tip:** Visit Ximending and the night markets in the evening for the best shopping and dining experience.

- **Don't Miss:** The panoramic views from Taipei 101, unique fashion finds in Zhongxiao Dunhua, and the street food delights of Shilin and Raohe night markets.

Exploring these shopping districts and dining spots provides a comprehensive taste of Taipei's vibrant culture, offering everything from high-end luxury to local street food and fashion.

CULTURAL AND HISTORICAL SITES

Taipei, the vibrant capital of Taiwan, is a treasure trove of cultural and historical sites that reflect the island's rich heritage. Here's a closer look at some must-visit landmarks that offer a deep dive into Taipei's past and present.

- **National Palace Museum**

Renowned for its vast collection of ancient Chinese imperial artifacts, the National Palace Museum is a cornerstone of Taipei's cultural scene. The museum's collection, amassed over centuries, includes over 700,000 pieces of art, ranging from calligraphy and paintings to ancient ceramics and jade. The museum is housed in a traditional Chinese-style building and offers an extensive overview of Chinese history, art, and culture. **Opening Hours:** Daily from 8:30 AM to 6:30 PM (extended hours on Fridays and Saturdays until 9:00 PM). **Admission:** NT$350 (USD 11) for adults.

- **Chiang Kai-shek Memorial Hall**

A symbol of Taiwan's political history, the Chiang Kai-shek Memorial Hall is dedicated to the former President of the Republic of China. The grand structure features a massive white marble hall with a blue-tiled roof and a towering statue of

Chiang Kai-shek. Visitors can witness the ceremonial changing of the guard, explore the surrounding gardens, and learn about Taiwan's modern history. **Opening Hours:** Daily from 9:00 AM to 6:00 PM. **Admission:** Free.

- **Longshan Temple**

Longshan Temple, located in the heart of Taipei's historic district, is one of the city's oldest and most famous temples. Built in 1738, the temple is dedicated to Guanyin, the Buddhist goddess of mercy. It showcases intricate wood carvings, vibrant murals, and traditional architecture, making it a focal point of Taipei's spiritual and cultural life. **Opening Hours:** Daily from 6:00 AM to 10:00 PM. **Admission:** Free.

- **Taipei City God Temple**

Situated in the bustling Ximending area, the Taipei City God Temple is another significant religious site. Dedicated to the City God, who is believed to protect the city's residents, the temple is known for its ornate decorations and lively atmosphere. It offers a glimpse into local religious practices and traditions **Opening Hours:** Daily from 8:00 AM to 10:00 PM. **Admission:** Free.

- **228 Peace Memorial Park**

This park commemorates the 228 Incident of 1947, a pivotal event in Taiwan's modern history. The park features historical monuments, including a large memorial monument and the 228 Memorial Museum, which provides insights into the incident and its impact on Taiwanese society. **Opening Hours:** Daily from 8:00 AM to 6:00 PM. **Admission:** Free.

- **Pro Tips & Don't Miss**

- **Pro Tip:** Consider hiring a local guide or joining a cultural tour to gain deeper insights into the historical significance of these sites.
- **Don't Miss:** The intricate details of Longshan Temple's carvings, the peaceful ambiance of 228 Peace Memorial Park, and the grand architecture of Chiang Kai-shek Memorial Hall. Each site offers unique perspectives on Taipei's rich cultural tapestry.

NIGHTLIFE AND ENTERTAINMENT

Taipei, the bustling capital of Taiwan, comes alive after dark with an array of vibrant nightlife hotspots. Here's a guide to some of the top districts where you can enjoy the best of Taipei's nightlife.

- **Xinyi District**

Xinyi District is Taipei's premier nightlife area, known for its upscale clubs, bars, and lounges. Located in the heart of the city, it's easily accessible via the Taipei City Hall MRT Station. Popular spots include:

- **Elektro:** A high-energy club with international DJs, located at ATT 4 FUN, No. 12, Songshou Road. **Opening Hours:** Friday and Saturday from 10:00 PM to 4:00 AM. **Admission Fee:** NT$800-NT$1,500. Tourists should look out for its impressive light shows and top-notch sound system.

- **Frank Taipei:** A stylish rooftop bar offering stunning views of Taipei 101, located at No. 12, Songshou Road, 10th Floor. **Opening Hours:** Daily from 6:00 PM to 2:00 AM. **Admission Fee:** Free, but drinks cost around NT$300-NT$500 each. Visitors should enjoy the crafted cocktails and panoramic city views.

- **Zhongshan District**

Zhongshan District is another popular nightlife destination, known for its diverse range of bars and live music venues. Accessible via Zhongshan MRT Station, key spots include:

- **Revolver:** A popular live music venue and bar located at No. 1, Section 1, Roosevelt Road. **Opening Hours:** Daily from 6:00 PM to 2:00 AM. **Admission Fee:** Free, but drinks cost around NT$200-NT$400. This spot is known for its live bands and laid-back atmosphere.

- **OMNI Nightclub:** One of Taipei's most renowned clubs, located at No. 2, Section 5, Zhongxiao East Road. **Opening Hours:** Friday and Saturday from 10:00 PM to 4:00 AM. **Admission Fee:** NT$800-NT$1,200. Look out for their spectacular light and sound systems and international DJ lineups.

- **Daan District**

Daan District is famed for its trendy bars and relaxed lounges, perfect for a laid-back night out. Easily accessible via Daan MRT Station, highlights include:

- **Taipei East District (東區):** Known for its trendy vibe and hip bars. Popular spots include the Barcode Taipei at No. 22, Songgao Road, **Opening Hours:** Daily from 6:00 PM to 2:00 AM. **Admission Fee:** Free, but expect to pay NT$300-NT$500 per drink. Visitors should try their signature cocktails and enjoy the sophisticated ambiance.

- **On Tap Taipei:** A British-style pub offering a variety of beers and pub food, located at No. 21, Section 2, Jianguo South Road. **Opening Hours:** Daily from 5:00 PM to 2:00 AM. **Admission Fee:** Free, with drinks ranging from NT$150-NT$300. A great place to catch live sports and enjoy a casual night out.

- **Pro Tips & What to Look Out For**

- **Pro Tip:** Dress smartly, especially for upscale clubs in the Xinyi District, as some places have a dress code.
- **Don't Miss:** The rooftop bars in Xinyi for amazing views, and live music nights at Revolver for a more relaxed vibe.

These nightlife hotspots offer a variety of experiences, from high-energy clubs to relaxed bars, ensuring that every visitor can find something to enjoy in Taipei's vibrant nightlife scene.

EIGHT

WHERE TO STAY: TOP ACCOMMODATIONS

LUXURY HOTELS

Taiwan offers a variety of luxury accommodations, providing guests with world-class amenities, impeccable service, and prime locations. Whether you're in the bustling city of Taipei or the serene countryside, these hotels promise an unforgettable stay.

Luxury hotels in Taiwan are often characterized by their sophisticated design, spacious rooms, and top-tier facilities such as spas, fine dining restaurants, and breathtaking views. Many of these hotels are conveniently located near popular attractions, making them ideal for travelers looking to explore the local culture while enjoying the highest standard of comfort.

Here are the top five luxury hotels in Taiwan:

- **Mandarin Oriental, Taipei**
- **Price Range:** NT$15,000 - NT$30,000 per night
- **Website:** Mandarin Oriental, Taipei - https://www.mandarinoriental.com/taipei/songshan-luxury-hotel
- **Address:** No. 158, Dunhua North Road, Songshan District, Taipei City 10548, Taiwan
- **Contact:** +886 2 2715 6888

The Mandarin Oriental, Taipei is a beacon of luxury in the heart of Taipei, offering elegantly designed rooms, an extensive spa, and gourmet dining options. Guests can enjoy proximity to Taipei Arena and the vibrant shopping district of Xinyi.

- **The Ritz-Carlton, Taipei**
- **Price Range:** NT$12,000 - NT$25,000 per night
- **Website:** The Ritz-Carlton, Taipei - https://www.ritzcarlton.com/taipei
- **Address:** No. 3, Section 2, Zhongxiao East Road, Zhongzheng District, Taipei City 100, Taiwan
- **Contact:** +886 2 2181 8888

This luxurious hotel offers spacious suites with stunning city views, a rooftop bar, and a world-class spa. Located near Taipei 101 and the National Palace Museum, it's a perfect base for exploring Taipei's top attractions.

- **W Taipei**
- **Price Range:** NT$10,000 - NT$20,000 per night
- **Website:** W Taipei - https://www.marriott.com/hotels/travel/tpewh-w-taipei/
- **Address:** No. 10, Section 5, Zhongxiao East Road, Xinyi District, Taipei City 110, Taiwan
- **Contact:** +886 2 7703 8888

W Taipei is known for its chic, modern design, and vibrant atmosphere. The hotel features a stunning outdoor pool, trendy bars, and is located just steps away from the Taipei 101 building and Xinyi shopping district.

- **The Lalu, Sun Moon Lake**
- **Price Range:** NT$18,000 - NT$40,000 per night
- **Website:** The Lalu - http://www.thelalu.com.tw/
- **Address:** No. 142, Zhongzheng Road, Yuchi Township, Nantou County 555, Taiwan
- **Contact:** +886 49 285 6888

Perched on the shores of Sun Moon Lake, The Lalu offers serene luxury with panoramic views, an infinity pool, and a focus on Zen-inspired design. The hotel is perfect for those looking to relax and enjoy the natural beauty of Taiwan.

- **Regent Taipei**
- **Price Range:** NT$9,000 - NT$18,000 per night
- **Website:** Regent Taipei - https://www.regenthotels.com/regent-taipei
- **Address:** No. 3, Lane 39, Section 2, Zhongshan North Road, Zhongshan District, Taipei City 104, Taiwan
- **Contact:** +886 2 2523 8000

The Regent Taipei combines luxury with comfort, offering a rooftop pool, a luxury shopping arcade, and multiple dining options. It's located near the Taipei Fine Arts Museum and the bustling Zhongshan shopping area.

These luxury hotels in Taiwan offer more than just a place to stay—they provide an experience that enhances any visit to this beautiful island.

BOUTIQUE VILLAS

For travelers seeking a more personalized and intimate experience, boutique villas in Taiwan offer a unique blend of luxury, privacy, and local charm. These accommodations often feature stylish interiors, personalized service, and exclusive locations that provide a distinct sense of place. Perfect for honeymooners, families, or anyone looking to escape the bustle of traditional hotels, boutique villas offer a home away from home with a touch of elegance.

Here are the top five boutique villas in Taiwan:

- **Villa 32**
- **Price Range:** NT$12,000 - NT$25,000 per night
- **Website:** Villa 32 - http://www.villa32.com/
- **Address:** No. 32, Zhongshan Road, Beitou District, Taipei City 112, Taiwan
- **Contact:** +886 2 6611 8888

Villa 32 is a luxurious retreat in the heart of Taipei's Beitou hot spring district. The villa offers five spacious suites, each uniquely designed with a blend of modern and traditional aesthetics. Amenities include private hot spring baths, a gourmet restaurant, and serene gardens. Nearby attractions include Beitou Hot Spring Museum and Yangmingshan National Park.

- **The Lalu Villas**
- **Price Range:** NT$18,000 - NT$40,000 per night
- **Website:** The Lalu - http://www.thelalu.com.tw/
- **Address:** No. 142, Zhongzheng Road, Yuchi Township, Nantou County 555, Taiwan
- **Contact:** +886 49 285 6888

Situated by the picturesque Sun Moon Lake, The Lalu Villas offer a serene and luxurious escape with stunning lake views. The villas feature minimalist design, private pools, and expansive living spaces. Guests can enjoy amenities like a spa, fine dining, and easy access to the lake's attractions such as the Wenwu Temple and Ita Thao Village.

- **Driftwood Villa**
- **Price Range:** NT$8,000 - NT$15,000 per night
- **Website:** Driftwood Villa - https://www.driftwoodvilla.com.tw/
- **Address:** No. 60, Shuqi Road, Shoufeng Township, Hualien County 974, Taiwan
- **Contact:** +886 3 867 2100

Driftwood Villa, located near Taroko National Park, offers a blend of rustic charm and modern comfort. Each villa is designed with natural materials and features private terraces overlooking the mountains. Amenities include an outdoor pool, in-villa dining, and guided tours. Nearby attractions include the Taroko Gorge and Qingshui Cliffs.

- **Adagio Reindeer Villa**
- **Price Range:** NT$6,000 - NT$12,000 per night
- **Website:** Adagio Reindeer Villa - https://www.adagio.com.tw/
- **Address:** No. 21-25, Wenhua Lane, Xinyi Township, Nantou County 556, Taiwan
- **Contact:** +886 49 291 3988

Nestled in the Alishan region, Adagio Reindeer Villa offers a peaceful retreat with stunning views of the surrounding tea plantations. The villas are cozy and elegantly decorated, with private gardens and terraces. Amenities include a tea room, yoga classes, and hiking trails. Nearby attractions include Alishan National Scenic Area and Fenchihu Old Street.

- **Cingjing Xiafei Music Villa**
- **Price Range:** NT$7,000 - NT$14,000 per night
- **Website:** Cingjing Xiafei Music Villa - https://www.xiafeivilla.com.tw/
- **Address:** No. 33, Rongguang Lane, Datong Village, Ren'ai Township, Nantou County 546, Taiwan
- **Contact:** +886 49 280 1166

Located in the Cingjing Farm area, this villa offers breathtaking mountain views and a musical theme. The spacious villas feature large windows, private balconies, and luxurious furnishings. Amenities include a restaurant, live music events, and guided tours. Nearby attractions include the Cingjing Skywalk and the Green Green Grasslands.

These boutique villas provide a unique and luxurious way to experience Taiwan, offering comfort, privacy, and proximity to some of the island's most beautiful and interesting locations.

COZY BED AND BREAKFASTS

Taiwan is renowned for its welcoming hospitality, and cozy bed and breakfasts (B&Bs) offer a homey alternative to larger hotels. These charming accommodations provide a personal touch, often run by local families who share insider tips and stories about the area. B&Bs are perfect for travelers looking for a warm and intimate stay, often with the added benefit of homemade breakfasts featuring local delicacies.

Here are the top five cozy bed and breakfasts in Taiwan:

- **Jing Guan Ming Lou Holiday Hotel**
- **Price Range:** NT$2,500 - NT$5,000 per night
- **Website:** Jing Guan Ming Lou - http://www.jingguanminglou.com.tw/
- **Address:** No. 30, Minzu Rd, Hualien City, Hualien County 970, Taiwan
- **Contact:** +886 3 833 5833

Located in Hualien, this B&B offers stunning sea views and is just a short drive from Qixingtan Beach. The rooms are elegantly decorated with a blend of modern and traditional Taiwanese elements. Amenities include free Wi-Fi, a communal lounge, and bike rentals. Nearby attractions include Taroko Gorge and Pine Garden.

- **Secret Garden B&B**
- **Price Range:** NT$3,000 - NT$6,000 per night
- **Website:** Secret Garden B&B - https://www.secretgardenbb.com.tw/
- **Address:** No. 9-1, Shizhuo, Alishan Township, Chiayi County 605, Taiwan
- **Contact:** +886 5 251 2112

Nestled in the Alishan Mountains, Secret Garden B&B offers a tranquil retreat surrounded by nature. Each room features panoramic mountain views and rustic décor. Guests can enjoy homemade breakfasts, a beautiful garden, and easy access to hiking trails. Nearby attractions include Alishan National Scenic Area and Fenchihu Old Street.

- **Moon Lake House**
- **Price Range:** NT$2,200 - NT$4,500 per night
- **Website:** Moon Lake House - http://www.moonlakehouse.com.tw/
- **Address:** No. 5, Zhongshan Road, Yuchi Township, Nantou County 555, Taiwan
- **Contact:** +886 49 285 5678

Situated near Sun Moon Lake, Moon Lake House offers cozy accommodations with beautiful lake views. The rooms are tastefully furnished, and the B&B provides a delicious breakfast featuring local ingredients. Amenities include free parking, a garden, and a terrace. Nearby attractions include Sun Moon Lake Ropeway and Wenwu Temple.

- **Simply Life B&B**
- **Price Range:** NT$1,800 - NT$3,800 per night
- **Website:** Simply Life B&B - http://www.simplylifebb.com/
- **Address:** No. 36, Ren'ai Road, Jincheng Township, Kinmen County 893, Taiwan
- **Contact:** +886 82 323 666

Located on Kinmen Island, Simply Life B&B offers a blend of modern comfort and historical charm. The rooms are spacious and well-appointed, and guests can enjoy a hearty breakfast each morning. Amenities include free Wi-Fi, bicycle rentals, and guided tours. Nearby attractions include Zhaishan Tunnel and Kinmen National Park.

- **Fun Relax B&B**
- **Price Range:** NT$2,000 - NT$4,200 per night
- **Website:** Fun Relax B&B - https://www.funrelaxbb.com/
- **Address:** No. 22-3, Quiche Rd, Jiufen, Ruifang District, New Taipei City 224, Taiwan

- **Contact:** +886 2 2406 1234

Perched in the picturesque town of Jiufen, Fun Relax B&B offers breathtaking views of the mountains and the sea. The rooms are cozy and well-furnished, reflecting the local culture. Guests can enjoy a traditional Taiwanese breakfast, a sun terrace, and easy access to the old street markets. Nearby attractions include Jiufen Old Street and the Gold Museum.

These cozy B&Bs provide a warm and intimate lodging experience, perfect for travelers looking to immerse themselves in Taiwanese hospitality while enjoying the local culture and attractions.

BUDGET-FRIENDLY OPTIONS

Traveling on a budget in Taiwan doesn't mean you have to sacrifice comfort or convenience. Taiwan offers numerous budget-friendly accommodation options, ranging from hostels to guesthouses, that provide clean and comfortable stays without breaking the bank. These places often come with essential amenities, friendly service, and easy access to local attractions, making them perfect for travelers looking to explore Taiwan affordably.

Here are the top five budget-friendly accommodations in Taiwan:

- **Star Hostel Taipei Main Station**
- **Price Range:** NT$700 - NT$1,500 per night
- **Website:** Star Hostel - https://www.starhostel.com.tw/
- **Address:** 2F, No. 50, Huayin St, Datong District, Taipei City 103, Taiwan

- Contact: +886 2 2550 5111

Located just a short walk from Taipei Main Station, Star Hostel offers a vibrant and welcoming atmosphere. The hostel features dormitory and private rooms, a spacious common area, a fully equipped kitchen, and free Wi-Fi. Nearby attractions include Ningxia Night Market and the Museum of Contemporary Art.

- **Flip Flop Hostel - Garden**

- Price Range: NT$600 - NT$1,200 per night
- Website: Flip Flop Hostel - http://www.flipflophostel.com/
- Address: No. 103, Huayin St, Datong District, Taipei City 103, Taiwan
- Contact: +886 2 2559 3666

Flip Flop Hostel - Garden, located in the heart of Taipei, offers a cozy and green environment. The hostel provides dormitory and private rooms, a garden, a communal lounge, and free breakfast. It's conveniently located near Taipei Main Station and the Q Square Mall.

- **Mini Voyage Hostel**

- Price Range: NT$500 - NT$1,000 per night
- Website: Mini Voyage Hostel - http://www.minivoyagehostel.com/
- Address: No. 100, Guolian 1st Rd, Hualien City, Hualien County 970, Taiwan
- Contact: +886 3 833 0313

Situated in Hualien, Mini Voyage Hostel offers stylish and clean accommodations with both dormitory and private rooms. The hostel features a communal kitchen, free Wi-Fi, and a lounge area. It's close to Hualien Railway Station, Dongdaemun Night Market, and Pine Garden.

- **FZ Hostel**

- Price Range: NT$600 - NT$1,200 per night
- Website: FZ Hostel - http://www.fzhostel.com/
- Address: No. 82, Linsen Rd, East District, Tainan City 701, Taiwan
- Contact: +886 6 221 9158

FZ Hostel in Tainan offers a blend of traditional and modern Taiwanese styles. The hostel includes dormitory and private rooms, free breakfast, a rooftop terrace, and a communal kitchen. It's near Tainan Railway Station, Chihkan Tower, and Shennong Street.

- **Banana Hostel**
- **Price Range:** NT$700 - NT$1,500 per night
- **Website:** Banana Hostel - http://www.bananahostel.com.tw/
- **Address:** 5F, No. 20, Ln. 30, Sec. 1, Xinsheng S. Rd, Da'an District, Taipei City 106, Taiwan
- **Contact:** +886 2 2394 2957

Located in Taipei's Da'an District, Banana Hostel offers a laid-back atmosphere with dormitories and private rooms. The hostel features free breakfast, Wi-Fi, a common lounge, and laundry facilities. It's close to Dongmen Station, Yongkang Street, and Daan Forest Park.

These budget-friendly accommodations provide excellent value for money, allowing travelers to enjoy Taiwan's rich culture, delicious food, and beautiful scenery without spending a fortune.

NINE

WHERE TO EAT: CULINARY DELIGHTS

GASTRONOMIC WONDERS OF TAIWAN

Taiwan is a culinary paradise, renowned for its vibrant street food, traditional dishes, and innovative cuisine. Travelers to Taiwan will find an abundance of flavors and textures, from savory snacks to sweet desserts, all reflecting the island's rich cultural heritage.

- **Beef Noodle Soup (牛肉麵)**
- **Description:** This iconic Taiwanese dish features tender chunks of braised beef, hearty noodles, and a flavorful broth made with soy sauce, garlic, and Chinese spices.
- **Recipe:** The broth typically includes beef bones, soy sauce, star anise, ginger, garlic, and various herbs. The beef is slow-cooked until tender, and the noodles are added just before serving.
- **Where to Find:** Lin Dong Fang Beef Noodles
- **Location:** No. 274, Section 2, Bade Road, Zhongshan District, Taipei City
- **Cost:** NT$150-NT$250 per bowl

- **Xiao Long Bao (小籠包)**
- **Description:** These delicate soup dumplings are filled with seasoned pork and a savory broth that bursts in your mouth with each bite.

- **Recipe:** The filling is made with ground pork, ginger, garlic, and a gelatinized broth that melts during steaming, creating a soup inside the dumpling.
- **Where to Find:** Din Tai Fung
- **Location:** No. 194, Section 2, Xinyi Road, Da'an District, Taipei City
- **Cost:** NT$200-NT$300 per basket

- **Oyster Omelette (蚵仔煎)**
- **Description:** A popular street food, this dish combines fresh oysters with a savory batter made from sweet potato starch and eggs, then topped with a tangy sauce.
- **Recipe:** Oysters are mixed into a batter of sweet potato starch and water, then fried with eggs and topped with a sweet and savory sauce.
- **Where to Find:** Shilin Night Market
- **Location:** No. 101, Jihe Road, Shilin District, Taipei City
- **Cost:** NT$50-NT$100 per omelet

- **Pineapple Cake (鳳梨酥)**
- **Description:** These traditional pastries have a buttery crust filled with sweet and tangy pineapple jam, making them a popular souvenir.
- **Recipe:** The dough is made from flour, butter, and sugar, while the filling consists of pineapple jam often mixed with winter melon.
- **Where to Find:** Chia Te Bakery
- **Location:** No. 88, Section 5, Nanjing East Road, Songshan District, Taipei City
- **Cost:** NT$30-NT$50 per piece

- **Bubble Tea (珍珠奶茶)**
- **Description:** Invented in Taiwan, this refreshing drink combines tea, milk, and chewy tapioca pearls, available in a variety of flavors.
- **Recipe:** Brewed tea is mixed with milk and sugar, then shaken with ice and tapioca pearls.
- **Where to Find:** Chun Shui Tang
- **Location:** No. 30, Siwei Street, West District, Taichung City
- **Cost:** NT$50-NT$80 per cup

Taiwan's culinary scene is a delightful journey through flavors and textures, offering something for every palate. Each dish tells a story of the island's history and culture, making dining in Taiwan a truly immersive experience. Whether you're exploring bustling night markets or dining in renowned restaurants, the gastronomic wonders of Taiwan are sure to leave a lasting impression.

WHERE TO EAT: DINING OPTIONS FOR EVERY PALATE

Taiwan is a food lover's paradise, offering a wide range of dining options from street food stalls to high-end restaurants. Each meal promises a unique taste of the island's rich culinary heritage.

- **Street Food Stalls**

- **Where to Eat:** Shilin Night Market, Taipei

- **Description:** Taiwan's night markets are legendary, and Shilin is among the most famous. Here, you can find a variety of local delicacies.

- **Top Foods:** Stinky Tofu, Oyster Omelette, Fried Chicken Cutlet

- **Cost:** NT$30-NT$100 per item

- **Pro Tips:** Arrive early to avoid long queues and bring cash as most vendors don't accept credit cards.

- **Traditional Taiwanese Restaurants**

- **Where to Eat:** Din Tai Fung, Taipei

- **Description:** Renowned for its precision and consistency, Din Tai Fung is a must-visit for dumpling lovers.

- **Top Foods:** Xiao Long Bao (soup dumplings), Shrimp and Pork Dumplings, Hot and Sour Soup
- **Cost:** NT$200-NT$500 per person
- **Pro Tips:** Make a reservation or be prepared for a wait, as this restaurant is very popular.

- **Seafood Restaurants**
- **Where to Eat:** Addiction Aquatic Development, Taipei
- **Description:** A modern seafood market with multiple dining options including sushi bars, hot pot, and seafood grills.
- **Top Foods:** Sashimi, Grilled Seafood, Seafood Hot Pot
- **Cost:** NT$300-NT$1000 per person
- **Pro Tips:** Visit during off-peak hours for a more relaxed dining experience.

- **Vegetarian Restaurants**
- **Where to Eat:** Yang Shin Vegetarian Restaurant, Taipei
- **Description:** Offering an extensive menu of vegetarian and vegan dishes, this restaurant is perfect for plant-based eaters.
- **Top Foods:** Vegetarian Dim Sum, Spicy Sichuan Tofu, Mushroom Hot Pot
- **Cost:** NT$300-NT$600 per person
- **Pro Tips:** Try their vegetarian dim sum for a unique twist on a classic favorite.

- **Cafés and Dessert Shops**
- **Where to Eat:** Ice Monster, Taipei
- **Description:** Famous for its shaved ice desserts, Ice Monster is a great spot to cool off and satisfy your sweet tooth.
- **Top Foods:** Mango Shaved Ice, Strawberry Shaved Ice, Milk Tea Shaved Ice
- **Cost:** NT$150-NT$300 per dessert
- **Pro Tips:** Share a large shaved ice with friends, as the portions are generous.

- **Signature Dishes and Recipes**
- **Stinky Tofu:** Fermented tofu that's deep-fried and served with pickled vegetables and a spicy sauce.
- **Xiao Long Bao:** Soup dumplings filled with pork and a savory broth.

- **Oyster Omelet:** A savory omelet made with fresh oysters, eggs, and a sweet and savory sauce.
- **Mango Shaved Ice:** A refreshing dessert made with finely shaved ice topped with fresh mangoes, condensed milk, and mango syrup.

- **Dining Tips**

- **Language:** While many restaurants in tourist areas have English menus, learning a few basic Mandarin phrases can be helpful.
- **Payment:** Cash is king at street food stalls and smaller eateries. Credit cards are accepted at larger restaurants and hotels.
- **Etiquette:** It's polite to wait for everyone to be served before starting your meal. Don't stick your chopsticks upright in your rice bowl, as this resembles funeral incense.

Exploring Taiwan's culinary delights is a journey through its culture and history, offering an unforgettable experience for every traveler

FINE DINING RESTAURANTS WITH SCENIC VIEWS

Taiwan offers an exceptional dining experience, where you can savor exquisite cuisine while enjoying breathtaking views. Here are some of the top fine dining restaurants with scenic views that you shouldn't miss:

- **The Top**
- **Price per Person:** NT$1500-NT$3000
- **Phone:** +886 2 2885 6288
- **Opening Hours:** 11:30 AM - 10:00 PM

- **Website:** The Top - http://www.thetop.com.tw
- **Physical Address:** No. 33, Lane 77, Section 2, Zhishan Rd, Shilin District, Taipei City
- **Overview:** Perched on the Yangmingshan mountainside, The Top offers a panoramic view of Taipei. The restaurant specializes in grilled dishes and hot pots, providing an excellent setting for romantic dinners and special occasions.

- **Silks Place Taroko**
- **Price per Person:** NT$2000-NT$4000
- **Phone:** +886 3 869 1155
- **Opening Hours:** 7:00 AM - 10:00 PM
- **Website:** Silks Place Taroko - http://www.silksplace-taroko.com.tw
- **Physical Address:** No.18, Tianxiang Rd., Xiulin Township, Hualien County
- **Overview:** Located within Taroko Gorge, Silks Place Taroko combines luxury and natural beauty. The restaurant offers a fusion of Western and Asian cuisine with stunning views of the surrounding marble cliffs and Liwu River.

- **Paris 1930**
- **Price per Person:** NT$3000-NT$5000
- **Phone:** +886 2 2175 5555
- **Opening Hours:** 6:30 PM - 10:00 PM
- **Website:** Paris 1930 - http://www.landishotelsresorts.com
- **Physical Address:** 5F, No. 41, Section 2, Minquan East Road, Zhongshan District, Taipei City
- **Overview: Paris 1930** at The Landis Taipei offers French haute cuisine in an elegant Art Deco setting. The rooftop restaurant provides a beautiful view of the city skyline, making it perfect for a luxurious dining experience.

- **YEN Chinese Restaurant**
- **Price per Person:** NT$2500-NT$4000
- **Phone:** +886 2 7703 8887
- **Opening Hours:** 12:00 PM - 2:30 PM, 6:00 PM - 10:00 PM
- **Website:** YEN Chinese Restaurant - http://www.wtaipei.com

- **Physical Address:** 31F, No. 10, Section 5, Zhongxiao East Road, Xinyi District, Taipei City
- **Overview:** Located on the 31st floor of the W Taipei, YEN Chinese Restaurant offers modern Chinese cuisine with spectacular views of Taipei 101 and the bustling Xinyi district. Dim sum and Peking duck are highly recommended.

- **Le Plage**
- **Price per Person:** NT$2000-NT$3500
- **Phone:** +886 3 888 1888
- **Opening Hours:** 12:00 PM - 2:00 PM, 6:00 PM - 9:00 PM
- **Website:** Le Plage - http://www.leplage.com.tw
- **Physical Address:** No. 30, Fude, Shoufeng Township, Hualien County
- **Overview:** Situated by the coast in Hualien, Le Plage offers fine dining with stunning ocean views. The restaurant focuses on seafood and local produce, providing a unique culinary experience.

- **Pro Tips**
- **Reservations:** Make reservations in advance, especially for weekend dining or special occasions.
- **Dress Code:** Some fine dining restaurants may have a dress code, so check ahead.
- **Special Requests:** If you have dietary restrictions, inform the restaurant when booking to ensure they can accommodate your needs.

Dining at these restaurants not only promises a delightful culinary experience but also offers the chance to appreciate Taiwan's scenic beauty from some of its most elegant dining venues.

CHARMING CAFÉS AND NIGHT MARKETS

Taiwan is renowned for its charming cafés and bustling night markets, each offering a unique and immersive culinary experience. Here are some of the must-visit spots:

- CHARMING CAFÉS

- **Fika Fika Café**
- **Price per Person:** NT$200-NT$400
- **Phone:** +886 2 2531 0908
- **Opening Hours:** 9:00 AM - 10:00 PM
- **Website:** Fika Fika Café - http://www.fikafikacafe.com
- **Physical Address:** No. 33, Yitong Street, Zhongshan District, Taipei City
- **Overview:** Known for its Scandinavian design and award-winning baristas, Fika Fika Café offers a tranquil atmosphere perfect for coffee aficionados. They serve freshly roasted coffee and homemade pastries.

- **Rufous Coffee**
- **Price per Person:** NT$150-NT$300
- **Phone:** +886 2 2732 2326
- **Opening Hours:** 8:00 AM - 10:00 PM
- **Website:** Rufous Coffee - http://www.rufous.com.tw
- **Physical Address:** No. 333, Section 1, Heping East Road, Da'an District, Taipei City

- **Overview:** A cozy spot known for its artisan coffee and friendly staff. The café also offers a selection of cakes and light meals.

- **Woolloomooloo**
- **Price per Person:** NT$250-NT$500
- **Phone:** +886 2 2721 8266
- **Opening Hours:** 7:30 AM - 10:30 PM
- **Website:** Woolloomooloo - http://www.woolloomooloo.com.tw
- **Physical Address:** No. 379, Section 4, Xinyi Road, Xinyi District, Taipei City
- **Overview:** Inspired by an Australian vibe, this café offers a variety of brunch options, coffee, and craft beers. The rooftop seating provides a great view of Taipei 101.

- NIGHT MARKETS

- **Shilin Night Market**
- **Price per Person:** NT$100-NT$300
- **Phone:** +886 2 2881 5557
- **Opening Hours:** 4:00 PM - 1:00 AM
- **Website:** Shilin Night Market - http://www.shilin-night-market.com
- **Physical Address:** No. 101, Jihe Road, Shilin District, Taipei City
- **Overview:** The largest and most famous night market in Taipei, known for its wide variety of street food, clothing, and accessories. Must-try foods include stinky tofu, oyster omelets, and fried chicken steaks.

- **Raohe Street Night Market**
- **Price per Person:** NT$100-NT$300
- **Phone:** +886 2 2769 8644
- **Opening Hours:** 5:00 PM - 12:00 AM
- **Website:** Raohe Street Night Market - http://www.raohe-night-market.com
- **Physical Address:** Raohe Street, Songshan District, Taipei City
- **Overview:** This night market is famous for its pepper buns and grilled squid. The Ciyou Temple at the entrance is a notable landmark.

- **Tonghua Night Market (Linjiang Street)**
- **Price per Person:** NT$100-NT$250
- **Phone:** +886 2 2706 2823
- **Opening Hours:** 6:00 PM - 12:00 AM
- **Website:** Tonghua Night Market - http://www.tonghua-night-market.com
- **Physical Address:** Linjiang Street, Da'an District, Taipei City
- **Overview:** A local favorite with a more relaxed atmosphere. Offers a variety of Taiwanese snacks, including pork buns and bubble tea.

- **Ningxia Night Market**
- **Price per Person:** NT$100-NT$300
- **Phone:** +886 2 2558 9710
- **Opening Hours:** 5:00 PM - 12:00 AM
- **Website:** Ningxia Night Market - http://www.ningxia-night-market.com
- **Physical Address:** Ningxia Road, Datong District, Taipei City
- **Overview:** Known for traditional Taiwanese dishes like oyster vermicelli and taro balls. The market has a nostalgic ambiance, reminiscent of old Taipei.

- **Pro Tips**
- **Timing:** Visit night markets early to avoid the crowds and enjoy freshly prepared dishes.
- **Cash:** Bring cash, as most vendors do not accept credit cards.
- **Food Sharing:** Try sharing dishes to sample a wider variety of foods.

- **Local Cuisine and Traditional Dishes to Try in Taiwan**

Taiwan's culinary scene is a delightful fusion of flavors influenced by Chinese, Japanese, and indigenous cuisines. Here are some must-try traditional dishes and local cuisine experiences in Taiwan:

- MUST-TRY DISHES

- **Beef Noodle Soup (牛肉麵)**
- **Overview:** This iconic Taiwanese dish features tender braised beef, hearty broth, and chewy noodles. It's a comfort food staple and a must-try for visitors.

- **Price per Person:** NT$100-NT$200

- **Stinky Tofu** (臭豆腐)
- **Overview:** A polarizing dish with a strong aroma, stinky tofu is deep-fried and served with pickled cabbage and spicy sauce. It's a popular night market snack.
- **Price per Person:** NT$50-NT$100

- **Oyster Omelet** (蚵仔煎)
- **Overview:** Made with fresh oysters, eggs, and a starchy batter, this savory dish is topped with a sweet and spicy sauce. It's a beloved street food.
- **Price per Person:** NT$60-NT$120

- **Xiao Long Bao** (小籠包)
- **Overview:** These delicate soup dumplings are filled with seasoned pork and hot broth, offering a burst of flavor with each bite. Din Tai Fung is a famous spot to try them.
- **Price per Person:** NT$150-NT$300

- **Braised Pork Rice** (滷肉飯)
- **Overview:** A simple yet flavorful dish, braised pork rice consists of minced pork belly simmered in a savory sauce, served over rice. It's a staple of Taiwanese home cooking.
- **Price per Person:** NT$50-NT$100

- RECOMMENDED RESTAURANTS

- **Din Tai Fung** (鼎泰豐)
- **Specialty:** Xiao Long Bao
- **Price per Person:** NT$300-NT$600
- **Phone:** +886 2 2321 8928
- **Opening Hours:** 10:00 AM - 9:00 PM
- **Website:** [Din Tai Fung - http://www.dintaifung.com.tw)
- **Address:** No. 194, Section 2, Xinyi Road, Da'an District, Taipei City

- **Liu Ping Xiao Guan** (劉品小館)

- **Specialty:** Beef Noodle Soup
- **Price per Person:** NT$150-NT$300
- **Phone:** +886 2 2578 3899
- **Opening Hours:** 11:00 AM - 10:00 PM
- **Website:** Liu Ping Xiao Guan - http://www.liupin.com
- **Address:** No. 12, Lane 26, Section 3, Minquan East Road, Zhongshan District, Taipei City

- **Lao Wang Ji Stinky Tofu** (老王記臭豆腐)
- **Specialty:** Stinky Tofu
- **Price per Person:** NT$50-NT$100
- **Phone:** +886 2 2555 1234
- **Opening Hours:** 5:00 PM - 11:00 PM
- **Website:** Lao Wang Ji - http://www.laowangji.com
- **Address:** Ningxia Night Market, Datong District, Taipei City

- **Abaoyu Oyster Omelet** (阿寶蚵仔煎)
- **Specialty:** Oyster Omelet
- **Price per Person:** NT$60-NT$120
- **Phone:** +886 2 2367 8901
- **Opening Hours:** 4:00 PM - 11:00 PM
- **Website:** Abaoyu - http://www.abaoyu.com
- **Address:** Shilin Night Market, Shilin District, Taipei City

- **Formosa Chang** (鬍鬚張)
- **Specialty:** Braised Pork Rice
- **Price per Person:** NT$50-NT$150
- **Phone:** +886 2 2778 5678
- **Opening Hours:** 10:00 AM - 10:00 PM
- **Website:** Formosa Chang - http://www.formosachang.com
- **Address:** No. 56, Section 1, Zhongxiao East Road, Zhongzheng District, Taipei City

- **Pro Tips**

- **Timing:** Visit popular restaurants early to avoid long waits.
- **Variety:** Night markets offer a wide variety of dishes, allowing you to sample multiple items in one visit.

HIDDEN GEMS FOR AUTHENTIC DINING EXPERIENCES

Hidden Gems for Authentic Dining Experiences in Taiwan

Taiwan's culinary landscape extends beyond well-trodden paths to reveal a range of hidden gems where you can experience authentic, local flavors. These lesser-known spots offer a glimpse into the island's rich food culture and are a must-visit for true food enthusiasts.

- Ningxia Night Market (寧夏夜市)

- **Location:** Datong District, Taipei City
- **Overview:** While not entirely off the radar, Ningxia Night Market is less frequented by international tourists compared to others. It's renowned for its traditional Taiwanese street food, including oyster omelets, stinky tofu, and pepper buns.
- **Must-Try: Beef Roll -** A savory pancake wrapped with beef, scallions, and hoisin sauce.
- **Price:** NT$50-NT$150 per item
- **Opening Hours:** 5:00 PM - 12:00 AM

- **Jiaoxi Hot Springs** (礁溪溫泉)

- **Location:** Jiaoxi Township, Yilan County

- **Overview:** Known for its hot springs, Jiaoxi also offers excellent local dining experiences. The town features numerous small eateries specializing in local delicacies such as wild boar meat and traditional Taiwanese porridge.
- **Must-Try: Wild Boar Meat -** Often prepared with a special sauce or as part of a stew.
- **Price:** NT$200-NT$400 per meal
- **Opening Hours:** Varies by restaurant

- **Lugu Township** (鹿谷鄉)
- **Location:** Nantou County
- **Overview:** Famous for its high mountain tea, Lugu offers dining experiences that highlight local produce, such as tea-smoked duck and wild mountain vegetables.
- **Must-Try:** Tea-Smoked Duck - Duck cooked with high mountain tea leaves for a unique flavor.
- **Price:** NT$300-NT$500 per dish
- **Opening Hours:** Varies by restaurant

- **Pingxi Old Street** (平溪老街)
- **Location:** Pingxi District, New Taipei City
- **Overview:** Known for its lantern festival, Pingxi Old Street features quaint shops and eateries serving traditional Taiwanese snacks. It's an excellent place to try unique local flavors like sweet potato balls and herbal soups.
- **Must-Try: Sweet Potato Balls -** Chewy and sweet, these are a popular snack.
- **Price:** NT$50-NT$100 per item
- **Opening Hours:** 10:00 AM - 6:00 PM

- **Tainan Anping Old Street** (安平老街)
- **Location:** Tainan City
- **Overview:** Anping Old Street is famous for its historical ambiance and local snacks, including shrimp rolls and peanut candy. It's less commercialized than other food districts, offering a more authentic experience.
- **Must-Try: Shrimp Roll -** A crispy, savory treat made with fresh shrimp.
- **Price:** NT$50-NT$150 per item
- **Opening Hours:** 10:00 AM - 5:00 PM

- **Pro Tips**

- **Local Insight:** Engage with locals to discover unlisted spots and hidden gems.

- **Timing:** Visit during off-peak hours to enjoy a more relaxed dining experience.

- **Exploration:** Walk through the areas to uncover street vendors and smaller eateries that might not be on the main maps.

These hidden gems provide a deeper connection to Taiwan's culinary traditions and offer a more personal and authentic dining experience.

TEN

PRACTICAL TIPS AND RECOMMENDATIONS

PACKING ESSENTIALS

When preparing for a trip to Taiwan, packing appropriately for the season is crucial to ensure comfort and convenience. Taiwan experiences a subtropical climate with distinct seasons, so here's a guide on what to pack based on different times of the year:

- **Spring (March to May)**
- **Light Jacket:** Spring temperatures are mild, but occasional rain showers make a light, waterproof jacket essential.
- **Layered Clothing:** Bring layers to adjust to varying temperatures throughout the day.
- **Comfortable Shoes:** Opt for waterproof or quick-dry shoes for exploring the city and countryside.
- **Umbrella:** Spring can be rainy, so a compact umbrella will come in handy.
- Sun Protection: Sunglasses and sunscreen are still necessary for sunny days.

- **Summer (June to August)**
- **Lightweight and Breathable Clothing:** Pack light, moisture-wicking clothes as temperatures can be quite high and humid.
- **Sun Protection:** Wide-brimmed hats, sunglasses, and high-SPF sunscreen are crucial to protect against strong UV rays.
- **Rain Gear:** A durable rain poncho or umbrella is essential as summer is the peak of the typhoon season.
- **Swimwear:** If you plan to visit beaches or hot springs, don't forget your swimwear.
- **Insect Repellent:** Mosquitoes are more active in the summer months.

- **Autumn (September to November)**

- **Layered Clothing:** Autumn can be a mix of warm and cool temperatures, so layered outfits are ideal.
- **Sweater or Light Jacket:** Pack a sweater or light jacket for cooler evenings and mornings.
- **Comfortable Footwear:** Good walking shoes are important for exploring cities and nature trails.
- **Sun Protection:** Continue using sunscreen and sunglasses for sunny days.
- **Rain Gear:** A compact umbrella or rain jacket is still useful as occasional showers are common.

- **Winter (December to February)**

- **Warm Clothing:** Although Taiwan has mild winters, bringing a warm jacket and thermal layers is advisable, especially in northern regions.
- **Rain Gear:** Winter can be wet, so pack a sturdy, waterproof jacket and a good umbrella.
- **Warm Accessories:** A hat, gloves, and scarf may be needed for cooler temperatures.
- **Comfortable Shoes:** Waterproof or water-resistant shoes are recommended for damp conditions.

- **General Essentials**

- **Travel Adapters:** Taiwan uses Type A and Type B plugs with a standard voltage of 110V.
- **Medication:** Bring any personal medications and basic first-aid supplies.
- **Reusable Water Bottle:** Stay hydrated while exploring.

Packing according to the season ensures that you remain comfortable and well-prepared for Taiwan's varied weather conditions, making your travel experience more enjoyable.

SAFETY AND EMERGENCY INFORMATION

When traveling to Taiwan, being prepared for emergencies and knowing how to access vital resources is crucial for a safe and enjoyable trip. Here's a guide to essential safety and emergency information for visitors:

- **Emergency Contacts**
- **Police:** 110. The primary contact for emergency situations involving law enforcement.
- **Fire Department and Ambulance:** 119. For immediate assistance with fire emergencies or medical emergencies requiring an ambulance.
- **Taiwan Tourist Police:** 02-2349-2111. A dedicated service for tourists that can assist with various issues and concerns.
- **Taiwan Centers for Disease Control:** 02-2395-1988. For health-related emergencies and disease control information.

- ONLINE RESOURCES AND APPS

- **Travel and Accommodation**
- **Booking.com:** booking.com - https://www.booking.com A comprehensive platform for booking hotels, hostels, and other accommodations in Taiwan.
- **Agoda:** agoda.com - https://www.agoda.com Offers a wide range of hotel options with user reviews and competitive pricing.
- **Hotels.com:** hotels.com - https://www.hotels.com Provides detailed hotel listings and often features special deals and discounts.

- **Budget Planning**
- **Trail Wallet:** trailwalletapp.com - https://trailwalletapp.com A user-friendly app for tracking travel expenses and budgeting.
- **Expensify:** expensify.com - https://www.expensify.com Helps manage and track expenses with receipt scanning and expense reporting features.

- **Dining and Local Experiences**

- **Google Maps:** google.com/maps - https://www.google.com/maps Essential for finding restaurants, cafes, and local attractions, with user reviews and ratings.
- **OpenRice:** openrice.com/taiwan - https://www.openrice.com/taiwan

A popular app and website for restaurant reviews and dining recommendations in Taiwan.
- **TripAdvisor:** tripadvisor.com - https://www.tripadvisor.com

Useful for discovering local attractions, dining options, and user-generated reviews.

- **Transportation and Exploration**
- **Taiwan Railway Administration (TRA):** [taiwanrailways.gov.tw - http://www.twtr.com.tw

For information on train schedules, ticket bookings, and station details.
- **Taipei Metro:** metro.taipei - https://www.metro.taipei

Provides metro routes, schedules, and fare information for Taipei's MRT system.
- **Uber Taiwan:** uber.com/tw - https://www.uber.com/tw

For convenient ride-hailing services in major cities across Taiwan.

By utilizing these resources and staying informed about emergency procedures, travelers can ensure a smoother and safer experience while exploring Taiwan.

USEFUL TAIWANESE PHRASES

Traveling in Taiwan can be a rewarding experience, especially if you're equipped with some key phrases and vocabulary to help you navigate daily interactions. Here's a guide to useful phrases for various aspects of your trip, including basic communication, dining, transportation, shopping, and emergencies.

- **Basic Taiwan Phrases**
- **Hello:** 你好 (Nǐ hǎo)
- **Goodbye:** 再見 (Zàijiàn)
- **Please:** 請 (Qǐng)
- **Thank you:** 謝謝 (Xièxiè)
- **Yes:** 是的 (Shì de)

- **No:** 不是 (Bù shì)

- **Excuse me:** 對不起 (Duìbùqǐ) / 不好意思 (Bù hǎoyìsi)

- **Do you speak English?:** 你會說英文嗎？(Nǐ huì shuō yīngwén ma?)

- **Dining and Food Phrases**

- **Menu:** 菜單 (Càidān)

- **I'd like to order:** 我要點菜 (Wǒ yào diǎncài)

- **How much is this?:** 這個多少錢？(Zhège duōshǎo qián?)

- **I'm vegetarian:** 我是素食者 (Wǒ shì sùshí zhě)

- **Spicy:** 辣 (Là)

- **Not spicy:** 不辣 (Bù là)

- **Can I have the bill, please?:** 可以給我帳單嗎？(Kěyǐ gěi wǒ zhàngdān ma?)

- **Transportation Phrases**

- **Where is the nearest MRT station?:** 最近的捷運站在哪裡？(Zuìjìn de jieyun zhàn zài nǎlǐ?)

- **How much is a ticket to [destination]?:** 到 [目的地] 的票多少錢？(Dào [mùdì dì] de piào duōshǎo qián?)

- **I need a taxi:** 我需要一輛計程車 (Wǒ xūyào yī liàng jìchéngchē)

- **Where is the bus stop?:** 公車站在哪裡？(Gōngchē zhàn zài nǎlǐ?)

- **Can you take me to this address?:** 你可以帶我去這個地址嗎？(Nǐ kěyǐ dài wǒ qù zhège dìzhǐ ma?)

- **Shopping Phrases**

- **How much is this?:** 這個多少錢？(Zhège duōshǎo qián?)

- **Can I try this on?:** 我可以試穿這個嗎？(Wǒ kěyǐ shì chuān zhèng ma?)

- **I'm just looking:** 我只是看看 (Wǒ zhǐshì kàn kàn)

- **Do you have this in a different size/color?:** 這個有其他尺寸/顏色嗎？(Zhè Ge yǒu qítā chǐcùn/yán sè ma?)

- **I'd like to pay by card:** 我想用信用卡付款 (Wǒ xiǎng yòng xìnyòngkǎ fùkuǎn)

- **Emergency Phrases**

- **Help!:** 幫忙！(Bāngmáng!)

- **I need a doctor:** 我需要醫生 (Wǒ xūyào yīshēng)

- **I'm lost:** 我迷路了 (Wǒ mílù le)
- **Call the police:** 打電話給警察 (Dǎ diànhuà gěi jǐngchá)
- **I lost my passport:** 我的護照丟了 (Wǒ de hù zhào diū le)

- **Other Important Phrases**

- **Is this place safe?:** 這個地方安全嗎？(Zhège dìfāng ānquán ma?)
- **Where is the nearest hospital?:** 最近的醫院在哪裡？(Zuìjìn de yīyuàn zài nǎlǐ?)
- **Can you help me find this address?:** 你能幫我找到這個地址嗎？(Nǐ néng bāng wǒ zhǎodào zhège dìzhǐ ma?)

By familiarizing yourself with these phrases, you can enhance your travel experience in Taiwan, making interactions smoother and more enjoyable.

LOCAL ETIQUETTE AND CUSTOMS

Understanding local etiquette and customs is essential for a respectful and enjoyable travel experience in Taiwan. Embracing these practices not only enhances your interactions but also fosters positive cultural exchanges. Here's a guide to key etiquette and customs in Taiwan.

- **Respect for Elders**

In Taiwanese culture, respect for elders is paramount. Always address older individuals with courtesy and deference. When greeting or interacting with elders, a slight bow or a respectful nod is appreciated. If you're in a group, allow elders to lead or sit first.

- **Politeness and Formality**

Taiwanese people value politeness and formality. Use formal language and titles when addressing strangers or business associates. Simple gestures like saying "thank you" (謝謝, xièxiè) and "please" (請, qǐng) are important in daily interactions. When handing or receiving items, including money, use both hands as a sign of respect.

- **Dining Etiquette**

Dining etiquette is integral to Taiwanese culture. Wait for the host to start eating before you begin. When dining, it's customary to use chopsticks properly and avoid sticking them upright in rice, as this resembles a funeral ritual. It's also polite to share dishes, so try a bit of everything on the table.

- **Dress Code**

Taiwanese dress modestly, particularly in temples and religious sites. It's advisable to dress conservatively, covering shoulders and knees. While casual attire is acceptable in most settings, smart casual wear is recommended for dining and business meetings.

- **Tipping**

Tipping is not customary in Taiwan and is not expected in most service settings, including restaurants and taxis. High-end establishments may include a service charge in the bill.

- **Public Behavior**

Public displays of affection are generally avoided in Taiwan. Maintain a calm and composed demeanor in public spaces. Loud conversations or actions may be considered impolite.

- **Visiting Temples**

When visiting temples, dress respectfully and remove your shoes if required. Keep your voice low and follow any specific instructions given by temple staff. It's customary to make a small donation if you're participating in a prayer or ceremony.

By adhering to these local etiquette and customs, you contribute to a respectful and immersive travel experience in Taiwan, aligning with the cultural norms and enhancing your overall visit.

SUSTAINABLE TRAVEL PRACTICES

Adopting sustainable travel practices is crucial for preserving Taiwan's natural beauty and cultural heritage. As a traveler, your efforts can contribute significantly to responsible tourism. Here are practical tips for traveling sustainably in Taiwan:

- **Reduce Plastic Use**

Minimize your plastic footprint by carrying a reusable water bottle, shopping bag, and utensils. Taiwan has a robust recycling system, so make use of recycling bins provided in public places. Opt for establishments that support eco-friendly practices and avoid single-use plastics whenever possible.

- **Choose Eco-Friendly Transportation**

Utilize Taiwan's efficient public transportation system, including trains, buses, and the metro, to reduce your carbon footprint. Taiwan's bike-sharing programs, such as YouBike, offer a convenient and eco-friendly way to explore cities. For longer distances, consider taking the high-speed rail (THSR) or regular trains instead of flights.

- **Support Local Businesses**

Boost the local economy by supporting small businesses, local markets, and restaurants. Choose accommodations that practice sustainability, such as those with energy-saving measures or waste reduction programs. Look for certifications or green labels that indicate an establishment's commitment to environmental practices.

- **Respect Natural Environments**

When visiting natural sites, stick to marked trails and avoid disturbing wildlife. Follow "Leave No Trace" principles by taking all your trash with you and avoiding picking plants or feeding animals. Respect local conservation efforts and adhere to guidelines set by national parks and natural reserves.

- **Participate in Community Initiatives**

Engage in community-based tourism that supports local conservation and cultural projects. Volunteer for beach cleanups, tree-planting events, or cultural preservation activities if available. This involvement helps foster positive interactions and contributes to the well-being of local communities.

- **Conserve Energy and Water**

Be mindful of your energy and water usage in accommodations. Turn off lights, air conditioning, and electronic devices when not in use. Take shorter showers and conserve water to help manage the environmental impact of your stay.

By incorporating these sustainable travel practices into your itinerary, you contribute to the preservation of Taiwan's environmental and cultural resources, ensuring that future generations can enjoy its unique offerings.

CONCLUSION

REFLECTING ON YOUR TAIWAN EXPERIENCE, ENCOURAGEMENT TO SHARE YOUR MEMORIES

As you reach the end of the Taiwan Travel Guide , it's time to reflect on the adventure that awaits you in this captivating island nation. Taiwan is a destination that combines breathtaking natural landscapes, rich cultural heritage, and vibrant modern experiences. Whether you're exploring the bustling streets of Taipei, relaxing by the serene waters of Sun Moon Lake, or marveling at the dramatic scenery of Taroko Gorge, Taiwan promises a journey filled with memorable moments and new discoveries.

From the historical depth of Taipei's National Palace Museum to the tranquil beauty of Alishan National Scenic Area, each location offers its unique charm and allure. The diversity of Taiwan's attractions ensures that every traveler can find something that resonates with their interests—be it hiking through lush forests, savoring exquisite local cuisine, or immersing yourself in the local culture at night markets and traditional festivals.

This guide has aimed to provide you with a comprehensive overview of Taiwan's highlights, practical travel information, and insider tips to enhance your experience. We've delved into the best times to visit, essential travel tips, and a detailed look at accommodations, dining, and transportation options. Our hope is that you feel well-prepared and excited as you embark on your journey through Taiwan.

Thank you for choosing this guide to accompany you on your adventure. It has been our pleasure to share insights and recommendations that will help you make the most of your trip. Taiwan's warm hospitality and stunning beauty are sure to leave a lasting impression, and we are honored to be a part of your travel experience.

As you explore Taiwan, we encourage you to share your memories and experiences with others. Your stories and photos can inspire fellow travelers and help spread the word about this incredible destination. Enjoy every moment of your trip, and let the experiences you gather enrich your life. May your time in Taiwan be filled with joy, discovery, and unforgettable moments.

Wishing you safe travels and a wonderful adventure in Taiwan!

Made in United States
Troutdale, OR
01/12/2025

27877287R00070